THE UMPIRE'S HANDBOOK

Revised edition

THE UMPIRE'S HANDBOOK

Revised edition

JOE BRINKMAN and
CHARLIE EUCHNER

THE STEPHEN GREENE PRESS
LEXINGTON, MASSACHUSETTS

First published in 1985 by The Stephen Greene Press, Inc.
This revised edition first published in 1987 by The Stephen Greene Press, Inc.
Published simultaneously in Canada by Penguin Books Canada Limited
Distributed by Viking Penguin Inc., 40 West 23rd Street, New York, NY 10010.

Library of Congress Cataloging-in-Publication Data

Brinkman, Joe.
    The umpire's handbook.
       1. Baseball—Umpiring. 2. Softball—Umpiring.
I. Euchner, Charlie. II. Title.
GV876.B75 1986   796.357′3   86-25771
ISBN 0-8289-0628-9

Printed in the United States of America
by The Alpine Press, Inc.
set in CG Century Schoolbook
by AccuComp Typographers
produced by Unicorn Production Services, Inc.

For Karen

Contents

Preface

A funny thing happened on the way to my publisher's. . . . I made a call at Fenway that says more about why *The Umpire's Handbook* can help aspiring umpires than just about anything else I could write about here.

Last night the California Angels—leading their division—came to Boston to meet the Red Sox, who are leading *their* division. Four hours and thirty minutes into the game, in the twelfth inning, just past midnight, with runners on second and third, the Angels brought in a new pitcher. I'm behind the plate, and it's been a long game, with a lot of pitches and a lot of pitchers—eleven, I think. The new pitcher comes in and hasn't even thrown a pitch yet, when he starts up with his right hand, stops, and steps off the rubber. I called a balk—to send in the winning run.

The call was a total reaction on my part. As an umpire, you just look for the pitches, you look for the plays, and you don't think about who's on base, who's hitting, who's pitching—you just react to things.

Naturally, the Angels went wild after that call; I had everybody on the field. But the rules say that if a pitcher starts up, stops, and then steps off the mound, it's a balk. The films showed that the pitcher *did* move his right hand, and I'm paid to make calls, so I did. That's what an umpire is.

Handling pressure is a real part of being an umpire. Making game-ending calls like last night's stays with you; you don't sleep as soundly as you would like to for a while. But the big thing is to try not to let it bother you. The guy who continues to umpire is the guy who can live with that; the guy who can't live with that is going to stop umpiring.

But what last night's call points out is just how important the role of the umpire can be. As I discuss throughout this book, the umpire has to be prepared and ready to make decisions that affect the outcome of a game. *The Umpire's Handbook* is meant to help prepare you for just this kind of situation. Of course, you need experience more than you need book learning, but a book can make you aware of situations you might have to cope with.

Just remember that you can't please everybody. Umpiring is not like being a politician; you can't tell everyone what they want to hear. You make a call the way you see it, and you can't make mistakes. I hope this book will help make you a better umpire.

Joe Brinkman
Lexington, Massachusetts
July 1986

Acknowledgments

Rookies need all the help and encouragement they can get from more experienced hands, whatever the business. This book is both authors' first foray into publishing. Our initiation would have been a lot tougher without the help and friendship of several people.

The book would not be possible at all without our agent, Richard Curtis, and our editors, Tom Begner and Kathy Shulga. Umpire Nick Bremigan's knowledge of baseball rules has always been invaluable, as has his friendship during the last several American League summers. Terry Allison's photography and Wayne Coffey's ideas add greatly to the book.

Others helped, notably American League umpire Rich Garcia, Ernie Whitt and Gino Petralli of the Toronto Blue Jays, and Stanley Bassin of California State Polytechnic Institute.

Warmest thanks are due Nancy Soderberg and Robert Goodell, great friends who never failed to keep things bright during the sometimes lonely grunt work on the manuscript.

A very special acknowledgment goes to Mr. Carl Childress of Edinburg, Texas, without whose technical editing this revised edition would not have been possible.

THE UMPIRE'S HANDBOOK

Revised edition

ONE
The Perils (and Rewards) of Umpiring

Baseball umpires do not usually attract much attention. Nor do they ever *want* to attract attention. The ultimate satisfaction for an umpire is to work a complete game without notice. When the players and fans pay attention to your performance, life tends to be difficult. Players talk to umpires only when they want to register a complaint. They never stop you as you trot to your position and say, "Hey, Joe, good call on that steal play. You were in great position. I admire the way you guys get on top of all those plays."

Since becoming a professional baseball umpire in the Class A Mid-West League in 1968, I have not always been able to avoid attracting attention. Let me explain. I played baseball, football, and basketball in college and in the military, so when I started umpiring I still had some very competitive instincts. That's why I probably set a record when I ejected twenty-six players and managers from games as a hotheaded rookie umpire.

The controversy did not end with that rookie year. Chances are I also set some kind of record when I refused to talk to Baltimore Orioles Manager Earl Weaver *for three years*; Weaver repeatedly attacked me in postgame interviews, and I decided the only way to get even was to give him the silent treatment. The press also puts me in the uncomfortable spotlight from time to time.

For about five years, the Boston sportswriters waged a battle with me that extended to the off-season. In one article about boxing, a *Boston Globe* sportswriter criticized the referee by saying he probably attended the Joe Brinkman Umpire School. I was in the headlines again in 1979 when I was one of the leaders of the major-league umpire strike.

With those few exceptions, though, I've managed to keep a reasonable distance from the game's spotlight. Until July 24, 1983, that is.

That is the date of the now-famous "Pine Tar Game" between the New York Yankees and Kansas City Royals at Yankee Stadium. As crazy as the game was—the incident became the *cause célèbre* for baseball in 1983 and eventually ended up in the state court system—the way the controversy developed tells a lot about the perils and satisfactions of working as an umpire, and about the fundamentals of good umpiring.

The Pine Tar Game consumed the average baseball fan's imagination more than any other umpiring decision in years. The armchair managers, umpires, and league presidents debated the implications of the ruling for weeks. I still get questions from fans about the decision.

Our decision certainly seemed unjust on the surface. We took away a home run in a crucial game from one of baseball's most popular players. We took it away for a nit-picking reason—he used too much pine tar on his bat handle. Sounds unjust, right? Well, we really had no choice in the matter.

The drama started in the ninth inning, with the Yankees leading the Royals 3–2. Both teams were in the middle of pennant races in their divisions in the American League. I can't say the game was more crucial to those teams' pennant chances than any other single game. But the game had an impact. The Yankees were riding high coming into the game, but lost thirteen of their twenty-two games after the incident. The incident's two principals—pitcher Rich (Goose) Gossage of the Yankees and third baseman George Brett of the Royals—went into protracted slumps after the game. Brett also complained about his golf game going bad.

With U. L. Washington on base for Kansas City, Brett stepped to the plate against Gossage, the Yankees' ace relief pitcher. When

Brett hit a 1-and-0 Gossage pitch into the right-field bleachers, everyone in The Bronx knew it was a home run that would give the Royals a 4–3 lead in the game. Everyone, that is, except the Yankees' feisty manager, Billy Martin, who was determined to teach aspiring umpires their first lesson.

Lesson Number One for Aspiring Umpires: Baseball is a "game of inches." The seemingly insignificant details of the game make the difference in many games. No play is so insignificant that it might not change the complexion of the game.

As Brett began his triumphant trot around the bases, Martin and Don Zimmer, a Yankee coach, started screaming at Yankee catcher Rick Cerone: "Look at the bat! Look at the bat!" Martin, Zimmer, and Cerone had apparently conferred before the game about protesting the other team's use of an illegal bat if that bat hurt them in a game.

Cerone at first threw the bat away, but then snatched it back from a bat boy when he realized that he was now the lead player in a great baseball drama. He showed the bat to our plate umpire, Tim McClelland.

Martin came out of the dugout to talk with McClelland. I knew Martin would try to convince us to nullify Brett's home run. Over the years, players have doctored their bats illegally to give them a little extra punch. A favorite trick is to drill a hole down the middle of the bat and fill it with cork, which gives the bat a jump from inside. Hitters also have put a hard wax or paraffin coating on their bats, which makes them harder. I also know of a minor-league player who once put a test tube filled with mercury in his bat. When he held his bat upright, the mercury did add to the bat's weight; when he swung, the mercury would fly toward the end of the tube in the barrel, greatly increasing the bat's potency.

Lesson Number Two for Aspiring Umpires: Do not allow the personalities of the players or managers to affect your decisions. Justice is blind. Remember the statue of the woman in front of the Supreme Court in Washington. She's blindfolded—she doesn't let any perceptions of the people in court affect her decisions.

Now, I'm not in love with Billy Martin. The man might be a baseball genius, as some people contend, but he also can be petty and unfair to his players and the umpires. Martin will do anything to win, no matter how it affects anyone else. He ordered his pitchers to throw spitballs as manager of the Detroit Tigers, and as manager of the Oakland A's, he overworked and ruined the arms of his pitchers—all in the interest of short-term gains. He has even less respect for umpires. He's always kicking and screaming. But you must forget about Martin's grating personality when you're working a game. You can't hurt him on calls just because he's not Mr. Congenial.

Martin said Brett hit the ball illegally because he had too much pine tar on his bat. Because the excessive pine tar made Brett's home run an illegally batted ball, Martin contended, the home run should be counted as an out—and the game should end with the Yankees the 3–2 victors. Battlin' Billy had waited for the perfect moment—an opposing player's heroic home run in an important game—to pull his little trick. It was a beaut.

Some people have asked me why we didn't notice Brett's excessive use of pine tar and declare the bat illegal *before* Brett hit the home run. If the issue had arisen before the stakes were so high—home run or out—there wouldn't have been a reason for the emotional outburst that followed. If Brett had been told to clean his bat or replace it with another bat, he would have done so happily.

But the umpire cannot check every aspect of the game before every pitch. If the umpire inspected the bat, ball, batter's box, coach's box, batting order, and so on, before every pitch, the game would take forever to complete. Preparing for every pitch would resemble the routine of a mother sending her child off to school for the first time. Because he has to concentrate on the action and keep the game moving at a brisk pace, the umpire sometimes has to depend on the players to point out some rule infractions. That's the case with excessive use of pine tar, and it's also the case in college and pro ball with claims of base runners failing to touch the bases.

The controversial substance at issue, pine tar, is sticky black gunk that players smear over their bat handles to get a better grip. The stuff smells just like the tar used to cover a driveway. Nobody would ever claim that a single application of pine tar on the bat's barrel improves the bat's potency; if anything, you'd think a ball that smacked against pine tar would stick to the bat, like in a cartoon. So why is the pine tar rule on the books? Some follow the reasoning of Calvin Griffith, longtime owner of the Minnesota Twins, who says that bats laden with pine tar ruin baseballs and therefore (gasp) increase the cost of maintaining a baseball supply.

A more likely rationale for the rule is that, if applied over a long period of time, pine tar could get into the grain of the wood, harden the bat, and increase its potency. The bat would cease to be completely wooden: it would have a hard outer shell that would give the batter an unfair advantage.

Lesson Number Three for Aspiring Umpires: Know the rule-book. You cannot be overruled by the league president for a judgment call, but you can be overruled for a rule interpretation.

Section 1.10 (b) of the official baseball rules for 1983 stated: "The bat handle, for not more than 18 inches from the end, may be treated with any material to improve the grip. Any such material, including pine tar, which extends past the 18-inch limitation, in the umpire's judgment, shall cause the bat to be removed from the game."

If that were the only rule concerning pine tar and its effect on the bat's legality, I probably would have told Brett to clean or get rid of his bat—but I would have allowed his home run to count. I would have told Martin to accept Brett's home run and go home. As Scarlett O'Hara said in *Gone With the Wind*, tomorrow is another day.

But there are two other rules involving pine tar and bats, and Billy Martin was only too happy to give me citations. Rule 2.00 states that an illegally batted ball is a ball hit with a bat that doesn't accord with Rule 1.10 (see above). And Rule 6.06 (a) states that a batter shall be declared out for hitting an illegally batted ball.

The rules as indicated above are no longer in the rulebook. Rule 2.00 is gone, and Rule 6.06 now refers only to a batter's stepping out of the box. Rule 1.10 (b) is now 1.10 (c).

Our umpiring crew that day—Drew Coble, Nick Bremigan, Timmy McClelland, and myself—huddled and debated the matter for a few minutes. The enormous amount of pine tar on Brett's bat and the string of rules left us with no choice but to call Brett out. If there was just a little too much tar, we might have been able to overlook it. But the pine tar was smeared all over the bat. So the pine tar reduced Brett's magnificent home run to an illegally batted ball. And an out.

It didn't seem right to take away Brett's homer because of a little pine tar, but rules are rules. Rules are all an umpire has to work with.

> *Lesson Number Four for Aspiring Umpires: Have enough knowledge and patience to explain your decisions to players and managers. Consider yourself an educator as well as an arbiter. You don't always have to explain, but you should always be prepared to.*

Once we reached our decision, we placed Brett's bat alongside home plate. The plate is seventeen inches wide, and it was obvious that the pine tar extended more than an inch beyond the plate's width. We correctly figured that the television cameras would show the scene, and the TV replays would help us explain the situation to the public.

When we made our painful decision, Timmy McClelland raised his right arm to signal that Brett was out. In retrospect, I think we should have called Royals Manager Dick Howser out on the field, before we announced our decision, to explain the situation. We could have told him about Martin's complaint about the pine tar and asked him to respond. That might have diffused the Royals' explosion after the decision.

> *Lesson Number Five for Aspiring Umpires: Think ahead. Before every game and before every pitch, try to anticipate which plays might develop. If you think about baseball as an umpire, rather than as a fan, you will react to plays on the field like an umpire.*

Like all good officials of the law, we had plenty of precedent to support our decision. The week before the Yankees–Royals game, in fact, we discussed how we might handle a possible pine tar dispute. Despite the popular perception that we were improvising with the rulebook, our decision at Yankee Stadium did not mark the first such pine tar ruling.

During another Yankees–Royals game in Kansas City a couple weeks before the Yankee Stadium fiasco, Yankee catcher Rick Cerone alerted umpire Rick Garcia about the excessive use of pine tar by—guess who?—George Brett. Nothing came of that complaint because Brett lined out. What's the point in nullifying an out and replacing it with another out? Garcia later warned Royals Manager Dick Howser about the consequences of the situation. So the Royals had had ample warning about their use of pine tar.

A few days before that incident, Cleveland Indians Manager Mike Ferraro asked us to call Jim Rice of the Boston Red Sox out because his bat had too much pine tar. We checked the bat and decided it didn't have too much gunk. Rice then switched bats and hit a double.

No hits were nullified in those cases because of pine tar. But the cases clearly proved that excessive use of pine tar is a reason for calling a batter out.

There were other precedents. In 1975, Thurman Munson of the Yankees was called out after hitting a single against the Minnesota Twins because his bat had too much pine tar; Bill Virdon, the Yankees' manager at the time, did not protest that decision. Later that year, John Mayberry of the Kansas City Royals was involved in another pine tar dispute. Pine tar rulings also reached down into the minor leagues. Players in the Class A New York–Penn League and the Class AAA Pacific Coast League also lost hits because of too much pine tar. Minor-league executives issued formal notices that supported the umpires' right to make pine tar decisions.

So we not only had the string of rules on our side. We also had plenty of precedents.

But precedents didn't mean much in our great pine tar controversy.

Lesson Number Six for Aspiring Umpires: Control the game; don't let the game control you. The umpire's main task is to maintain order on the field.

The reaction to our decision to nullify the home run was, predictably, outrage. George Brett stormed to the field to—well, I don't know exactly what he planned to do. He ostensibly came out to dispute the ruling, but he looked more like he wanted to kill the ump. He was a madman. I can still see his bulging eyes and red face. I ended up restraining Brett from behind; I don't know what he would have done if we had not blocked his mad charge.

As Brett argued his case, other Royals players sought to steal the evidence. Gaylord Perry, who has been known to do some illegal things with baseballs in his time, grabbed the bat and took off for the Kansas City clubhouse. The bat was passed down a chain of Royals until it ended up in the runway between the Royals dugout and clubhouse. Before long, I found myself in that runway trying to get the bat. I eventually grabbed Exhibit A and sent it to American League President Lee MacPhail, who was responsible for considering the inevitable protest by the Royals.

> *Lesson Number Seven for Aspiring Umpires: Always realize that you are the league president's representative on the field. The decisions you make have the full authority of the league office.*

Well, maybe that lesson doesn't always hold, but it should. MacPhail took three days to consider a protest lodged by the Royals. He concluded that our ruling was "technically defensible," but not in the "intent or spirit" of the rules governing pine tar. Because pine tar does not necessarily improve the bat's potency, MacPhail said, the Brett home run should count and the Yankees and Royals should meet again to complete the game. The Royals, 3–2 losers only days before, were now leading the Yankees 4–3 with two outs in the top of the ninth. The game was becoming a long-running soap opera.

The controversy continued. The Yankees and their celebrity lawyer, Roy Cohn, went to court to prevent the completion of the game. Justice Orest V. Maresca of the New York State Supreme Court issued an injunction against the game's completion. But just hours before the game's scheduled completion, Justice Joseph P. Sullivan of the Supreme Court's Appellate Division lifted the injunction. His decision stated, in part: "Play ball!"

George Steinbrenner, the Yankees' owner who up to this point had not been much of a supporter of umpires, assailed MacPhail's decision and predicted that the umpires' authority would be gravely undermined by MacPhail's decision. Billy Martin echoed Steinbrenner's sentiments: "The guy [MacPhail] made a joke of the rulebook."

The media, meanwhile, went berserk. The usually staid *New York Times* put its Pine Tar Game story on the front page alongside pieces about the weightier issues of war and peace. Other newspaper reporters and television commentators carried on for days about the "sticky situation" that came to be known as "Tar Wars." The decision even attracted comment in the most venerable of American institutions, the funny pages. In the comic strip *B.C.*, one cave man approached another who was seated behind a rock marked "Exterminator." The first man asked, "How do I get rid of bats?" The second man's answer: "Get some pine tar and exceed the eighteen-inch limit."

Eventually, the Yankees and Royals met at Yankee Stadium to complete the game. Five hundred fans—one wag said they were all law school students—journeyed to the stadium at dinnertime to watch a little more than a half-inning of baseball on August 18. The game did not end before some more theatrics from Billy Martin.

Because my umpiring crew was working an Angels game in California at the time, the American League assigned a different crew to work the game's completion. Dave Phillips was the crew chief.

When the game resumed with two outs in the top of the ninth inning, Martin ordered his players to make an appeal play at first base; when that appeal failed, the Yankees tried another appeal play at second base. Martin claimed that U. L. Washington and George Brett failed to touch all the bases on the Brett home run and therefore should be called out. Even if Washington and Brett had touched the bases, Martin said, that day's umpires had no way of knowing. Martin thought he had us trapped—again.

Lesson Number Eight for Aspiring Umpires: Intently watch everything that happens on the field. When the second baseman makes a force play, make sure he's in complete control of the ball. When a base runner rounds the bases, make sure he touches all the bases. Let no detail escape you.

Dick Butler, the supervisor of umpires for the American League, had heard barroom rumors in New York that Billy Martin was planning such a trick, so we had prepared ourselves. The umpires in my crew—who had watched both Washington and Brett touch all the bases—signed affidavits attesting to the fact. When Martin tried his appeals and then claimed that the new umpires could not make a ruling because they had not seen the earlier part of the game, Phillips showed Martin the papers. The affidavits were proof that the umpires had watched the base runners touch all the bases. There was nothing Martin could do. The pine tar shenanigans were over.

The Royals went on to win the game, 4–3.

Obviously, not everything worked out for my umpiring crew during the Pine Tar Game. Some of the lessons for aspiring umpires that I include in my account of the game have an ironic edge. But those lessons are all still valid. Maybe we should just add a ninth lesson: "Things do not always work out as they should."

We did all that we could during the Pine Tar Game. We made close to 400 calls that day as a crew. We watched each play carefully. We dealt firmly but respectfully with the members of both teams. We knew the rules and applied them as they had been consistently applied before. We anticipated game situations and didn't let personalities affect our decisions. We worked together, supported each other, and represented the league well.

We were overruled by our own league president—not on the basis of the rules and a significant history of rule enforcement—but on the basis of the "spirit" of the rules. We were demoralized by the president's decision.

The league president's decision was, we thought, just one of many examples of umpires being blamed for doing their jobs. It's the familiar "kill-the-messenger" routine. Some would even say that MacPhail's decision—along with a host of other indignities that umpires must endure—makes umpiring a losing proposition. You sometimes have to wonder if the umpiring profession can recommend itself to anyone but masochists.

But I know better than to allow umpiring's hassles to obscure its rewards. That's what I'd like to talk about.

Every January, I see firsthand evidence of the dreams that people of all backgrounds hold for umpiring. Some 200 to 300 young men and women travel from all over the United States and countries like Japan, South Korea, and Canada to enroll in organized baseball's two major umpire schools, which are owned and operated by me and National League umpire Harry Wendelstedt. The schools, created just after World War II, have graduated almost all of the 60 major-league umpires and 170 minor-league umpires now active.

The students at the two schools come from all kinds of backgrounds. We have enrolled a retired sixty-year-old optometrist, a twenty-one-year-old grocery bagger, a high-school social studies teacher, a bar bouncer, and a newspaper reporter. We have also enrolled a civil service worker from Los Angeles, retired professional football and baseball players, umpires from the professional league of Japan, and a former hot-walker from the Saratoga Race Track in New York State.

The way the students work their way through the five-week umpiring courses tells me a lot about the rewards of umpiring.

Many of the students come to the school with just an average fan's view of baseball; they leave as alert students of the game's fine points. Many come to the school with an intangible desire to stay involved in the game they have loved all their lives; they leave with the ability to stay in the game for the rest of their lives. And many students come to the school with little experience dealing with other people in pressure situations; they leave with the satisfaction that they can actually *take charge* of the players and the operation of a game.

In its own way, then, umpiring can be the most satisfying of pastimes.

Only one or two students in each year's classes will be lucky enough to ever make it to the major leagues' umpire corps. The rest either spend their summers languishing in the minor leagues, or they return home.

These students almost always come to the school with major-league aspirations, but umpiring offers them many rewards regardless of whether or not they go all the way. I enjoy my job as a major-league umpire, but I often wonder if the students who don't get a chance at umpiring in professional baseball truly *are* the lucky ones.

The students who don't get offers to work in professional baseball have a lot of advantages. For one thing, they can lead normal lives. They can go home and start other careers. They can get married without worrying about their personal relationships being strained by seven months of life on the road. They can actually *see* their spouse or friends once in a while.

And they can continue to be umpires.

While professional baseball offers but a few opportunities for umpiring, thousands of amateur leagues offer satisfying part-time work. Practically every community has a Little League Baseball organization for youngsters in elementary to high school. Most communities offer older players Connie Mack and Babe Ruth Leagues. Semi-professional leagues are thriving from Anchorage, Alaska, to Tyler, Texas. Every county in the United States has a high-school league. And softball leagues have grown at an unprecedented rate.

Officials for the United States Baseball Federation estimate that some 9 or 10 million youths play ball in amateur leagues. The National Federation of State High School Associations estimates that another 500,000 play baseball in interscholastic leagues. And the Amateur Softball Association of America reports that there are 173,000 teams and almost 4 million players in its leagues.

These leagues need umpires to call the games. Estimates vary, but most think there are well over 1.5 million umpires now working in the United States. That umpiring corps turns over rapidly. There is always room for a qualified newcomer to the profession. If you become an umpire, the rewards you reap will be far greater than the sacrifices you make.

Welcome to the profession. And don't blanch when the players and fans go into their routine from the 1955 Broadway musical *Damn Yankees*: "You're blind, ump! You're blind, ump! You must be out of your mind, ump. . . ."

TWO
What It Takes to Be an Umpire

"Reputation," says Iago, the bad guy in William Shakespeare's play *Othello*, "is an idle and most false imposition, oft got without merit and lost without deserving. You have lost no reputation at all unless you repute yourself such a loser."

Regardless of whether you agree with Iago's cynicism, the adage that "the reputation precedes the man" holds as true in umpiring as in any profession. The reputation might be fair or unfair, but it exists nonetheless. It's up to the umpire to make sure, every day, that he *deserves* a good reputation.

A frequent topic of conversation among players and coaches, the aspiring umpire will be either happy or dismayed to learn, is the quality of the league's umpires.

In many leagues, the umpires' records for throwing players out of games are as well known as the players' batting averages and earned-run averages. The stories about the umpires' rules decisions are passed on along with the stories about a hitter's 400-foot home runs or nineteen-strikeout performances. One umpire might have a reputation for being indecisive in making calls, while another could be known for his "quick gun." Some umpires are known as intellectuals—those who seem to know the rulebook as well as Thomas Jefferson knew the Constitution. Others are teachers—the guys who can explain game situations better than others.

The prerequisites for a good baseball umpire—and the ingredients of a good reputation—are varied. An umpire must be decisive, objective, consistent, and courageous. An umpire must hustle, anticipating what will happen during a play. An umpire must be a disciplinarian, but must also be understanding about players' frustrations and be willing to accept pointed criticism. He must also, from time to time, listen to players and coaches and, occasionally, teach them a thing or two.

In short, an umpire must have all the qualities of an Eagle Scout, right on down to "thrifty, brave, clean, and reverent."

The physical requirements

Eyesight

The making of a good umpire starts with several physical traits.

Eyesight, of course, is the major prerequisite. In the old days, before the dawn of the contact lens, no umpire would dare walk on a baseball diamond unless he had perfect 20/20 vision or the guts to deal with the consequences of lesser eyesight. When an umpire worked a game wearing eyeglasses, the players and fans ridiculed him endlessly after a controversial play. The goggle-clad umpire could make all the right calls and show perfect composure, but he was a marked man. He might as well put a target on his chest.

Now umpires are not at all reluctant to work a game as long as they have 20/20 *corrected vision.* Thanks to the undetectable contact lenses, nobody knows or cares whether the umpire needs a little help with his eyesight. Even umpires who wear glasses escape pot shots these days; many players, after all, also have shed their insecurities and have begun wearing glasses themselves. So the vision problem has all but disappeared in baseball.

But I am not so sure we should stop worrying about eyesight once we learn that we have the equivalent of 20/20 vision.

Perhaps because it's easy to ask someone to read what's on a chart of letters, many organizations do not pay enough attention to the more complicated eye skills. But these other skills such as *dynamic visual acuity, peripheral vision, depth perception,* and *visual pursuit* are the most important attributes of an umpire.

Studies of human development show that only about half of the people with perfect 20/20 vision are able to use their eyes together as a team. They do not have the visual pursuit, the fixation, or fusion—call it what you will—to use both eyes to their maximum benefit. The poor development of other eye skills also hampers the "perfect" 20/20 eyesight.

Think about depth perception. Depth perception is the ability to judge distances with your eyes. The automobile driver needs depth perception to judge whether or not he will hit another moving car. The construction worker needs depth perception to see whether the heavy machinery he uses puts things together correctly. And the baseball umpire needs depth perception to judge the distances of baseballs, bats, and players at a given time.

The home plate umpire must make between 270 and 300 ball-strike calls per nine-inning game. The pitches he watches move at speeds of seventy to ninety miles an hour. Now, no mere mortal can watch the pitch's entire movement. What the batter, catcher, and umpire do is "track" the pitch. They watch the pitch as much as they can, and make their judgments about the pitch on the basis of its "afterimage." The afterimage is the momentary picture you have of an object after looking away. For example, when you look at a light bulb and then look away, you have an afterimage of the bulb.

The umpire is in a much better position to judge the pitch's high speeds than either the batter or catcher. The batter has to decide whether to swing, so he makes his judgment of the pitch before it's even halfway to the plate. The catcher has a little more time to react. The umpire can wait for the pitch to travel its entire path before he decides whether it's a ball or strike. The extra quarter-second he has in invaluable. The umpire also has the advantage of using both his eyes to focus on pitches, while batters in the normal sideways stance depend more on one eye.

But still, life ain't easy for the umpire. The different speeds of the pitches can throw not only the hitter but also the umpire off stride. That ball could be moving straight into the strike zone, but the chances are it's going to dance around a bit. As the ball makes this journey, the pitcher, catcher, and batter are also moving around. One of the players might bump you during the pitch, and there's probably an infielder or base runner in the background to provide another dash of distraction.

Even though the umpire's job is easier than the batter's, the umpire must be able to do more than read an eye chart. He has to judge how the movement and changing distances will all come together. He needs depth perception.

I don't think I appreciated the importance of complete eyesight until a sixty-year-old optometrist named Rene Desaulniers attended the umpire school in 1983. I took for granted the various visual skills I possessed. Dr. Desaulniers has been an umpire in amateur leagues for thirty years, and he came to the school with ambitions not to become a major-league umpire but simply a better amateur umpire. Before he graduated, he set the school's instructors and students straight about the importance of good vision.

Many people get proper eye examinations only after experiencing physical discomfort they think might be related to poor eyesight. Some of the classic symptoms of eye stress include headaches, backaches, excessive sensitivity to light, car sickness, double vision, squinting, insomnia, loss of appetite, and an overall lack of energy. If you have any of those problems, you should get to the eye doctor right away. Even if you don't have those problems, you should take an eye exam at least once every year.

The American Optometric Association has published a "backgrounder" on sports vision. The booklet lists several abilities that people involved in sports need for peak performance. Among those abilities:

- *Dynamic visual acuity.* This ability allows you to not only see a ball or a player, but to see them when they're moving around. It enables you to move your eyes rather than your body to see a play.

    Without this ability, an umpire would have to move physically to follow a moving object such as a ball or a base runner. Of course, everyone has dynamic visual acuity. Without it, no one would be able to drive a car or watch a play, let alone assess the high-speed action in a baseball game. The level of this skill varies greatly from person to person. As an umpire, you should work to improve your dynamic visual acuity as much as possible.

    Optometrists can tell you about drills to test and improve your dynamic visual acuity. Talk to one.
- *Peripheral vision.* The ability to see activity ahead of and around you simultaneously. This skill is especially important

for the field umpire, who has to assess the entire field situation in order to get into position for a play. If a base runner attempts to tag up and score on a long fly ball, the umpire has to watch the outfielder catch the ball and the runner tag up at the same time.

The amateur-league umpire has to worry about his peripheral vision more than his counterpart in the major leagues, because he must cover more ground on the field. He must know what's happening all over the diamond, because there are fewer umps on the field.

You can do a simple drill at home to improve your peripheral vision. Sit in a chair and look straight ahead at an object. Have a friend use a slide projector to flash letters or numbers on each side of you. Try to identify the letters or numbers. When you can identify them, have your friend move them further away from the center object. When you can identify the letters again, move them out even further. This exercise would work really well if you could place two TVs at the far sides of your visual field.

- *Depth perception.* The ability to judge the distance between oneself and other objects—such as the ball, foul lines, and players. Depth perception enables the umpire to get in the right position to see plays without bumping into players or getting hit with balls.

  Depth perception means getting both of your eyes to work together. Eyeglasses often can help the eyes to work together by correcting nearsightedness or farsightedness. The "lazy eye" condition—one eye focuses on objects and the other eye fails to do so—is more difficult to correct. Many eye doctors say you *can't* fix a lazy eye after the age of five or six, but research is underway for correcting the lazy eyes of adults.

- *Visual pursuit.* The ability to use eyes to follow an object from its point of origin to its final destination.

  The plate umpire must be able to "track" pitches as they move from the pitcher's hand to the plate. Of course, the umpire needs to judge only where the ball ends up in the plate area, but seeing the whole pitch helps him anticipate what might happen when the pitch arrives at the plate. The field umpire has to watch players go after flies, apply tags, and so forth.

- *Eye-hand-foot-body coordination.* The ability to use the eyes as part of a complete physical system. The brain must record information from the eyes and coordinate that information with the rest of the body.

The best place to start when you get an eye examination is with *acuity*, the ability to see objects from certain distances (optometrists measure this with the familiar eye chart). Umpires should have 20/20 corrected vision. But the umpire should also have his other eye skills tested.

Conditioning

The umpire also must be in good physical shape. Baseball is a game that has more than its share of lulls, but the plays that develop are often explosive. Today's baseball players at all levels are an increasingly fit group. They move quickly, and the umpires have to move quickly to keep up.

If the players aren't as quick and agile as they are at the high school and college levels, they are inexperienced and prone to mistakes. Nothing typifies a Little League game as much as the outfielder throwing the ball to the wrong base or the shortstop overthrowing the ball to first base on a routine grounder. That's not criticism. Youth leagues are set up so that youngsters have a place to improve their skills. It just means that the umpires have to move around the field even more since the game is not very predictable.

One of the most frustrating aspects of umpiring is the image of a bunch of pot-bellied guys who call games because they aren't athletic enough to play the game. You watch televised baseball games, where some of the umpires are bulging out of their shirts, and you get the idea that only Ralph Cramdens need apply for the arbitrating jobs.

Some major-league umpires are in bad physical condition. They can get away with poor physical conditioning because there are four umpires working every game. They also get away with limited mobility because they know the game so well: anticipating what's going to happen where is second nature to them. But most of the amateur and professional leagues can't afford to pay more than two umpires a game. Umpires working under the two-man system have to do as much running as the players. They had better be in shape.

You don't have to be an Olympic athlete to keep up with the

players. I don't think an umpire will run more than one mile during a typical game. But the umpire must be quick. He must be able to pivot to switch direction quickly—turn on a dime and get to the other side of the diamond in an instant.

The plate umpire also must have strong legs to deal with the up-and-down pressure of squatting behind the plate. The constant stooping and standing affects your physical comfort. If you can't be comfortable behind the plate, your attention will wander. You won't see plays as well.

In the next chapter I've outlined a set of exercises that I suggest umpires do before every game to stay limber. But that's not enough. You should try to stay active off the field as well.

The other traits of the umpire

Once you're in good physical shape and you're confident about your eyesight, it's time to think about attitudes and some other more or less *learned* traits you need to be a good umpire. People in every profession, really, need to possess these traits.

When you take the field, think of yourself as a business executive. Your job is to manage the game the same way an executive would manage his office—keeping people busy, making snap judgments about the kind of jobs people are doing, settling disputes, avoiding problems before they happen, explaining ideas to people. If you do your job right, you'll get the same feeling of satisfaction that the executive gets when he sees the arrows on the sales charts pointing upward.

Here is a brief rundown of some of those traits you'll need as the baseball game's field executive.

Professional appearance and demeanor

When you arrive at the ballpark, be well dressed and act like a professional.

Umpires in most leagues wear well-pressed dark blue or gray slacks, a light blue collar shirt, and a dark blue baseball cap. Some umpires still wear a dark tie, but it's not necessary. There are variations on this uniform. In chilly weather, some umpires wear a dark blue blazer or sweater. American League umpires wore bright red sportscoats during foul weather until someone realized how much we looked like Captain Kangaroos.

Whatever the variations, the two umpires who work together should dress alike. The umpiring crew should look and act like a team throughout the game.

Different caps for the field and home plate are available. The plate umpire's hat has a shorter bill, which allows the plate umpire to pull the mask off his head without ripping the hat off as well. Try to get one of these hats. Wearing the long-billed hat backwards, like the catcher, when you're behind the plate looks unprofessional.

Use a dark leather belt, and wear dark, preferably black, athletic shoes.

The purpose of dressing well is to stress your professionalism. You also need to have the demeanor of a professional to gain the respect you need to call a game.

When you go to a game, concentrate only on the job at hand. Do not carry on extensive social conversations with the fans, players, or coaches. You should be courteous to the game's participants, and the home plate umpire should establish a good working relationship with the coaches and players, particularly the pitchers,

When the umpire takes the field, he should look like a professional. That means dressing in clean, pressed clothes that match your partner's. A good appearance shows the teams you mean business.

catchers, and batters. Between innings, don't talk with your partner; just stand alone. Don't leave the field—your job, after all, is to get the game under way again as soon as possible.

Hustle and decisiveness

There is one sin for which the umpire should not be forgiven: the lack of hustle. Both teams depend on the umpires to at least *try* to be in position to cover all of the game's plays. Mistakes will happen, but when the umpire does not try to avoid them he is doing everyone in the ballpark a disservice. It's not necessary for the umpire to huff and puff his way around the field if he can anticipate where a play might develop. He should just make sure he's on top of the play when it happens.

The umpire must also be decisive. When you make a call, make sure everyone in the park knows what it is. Make your signal obvious and bark out your calls in a crisp voice. When players or coaches complain about a call, allow them to make a brief case but don't let them ruin the game's flow by arguing all afternoon.

Make sure everyone in the ballpark—and for that matter, the folks over in the next county—understand your calls. A good, crisp call on a close play shows people you're confident of your judgments.

If a relief pitcher is dawdling, or if a team takes too much time between innings, ask them to please hurry it up.

Everyone responds well to a quick game. The players get in their grooves and are better able to react to the game's pace. The pitcher can get into a comfortable groove, fielders are more alert, and the batter is forced to concentrate better when the game moves swiftly. Whenever you get a pitcher or batter who takes a lot of time in between pitches, all the players seem to lose their competitive edge. Don't let it happen.

Try also to have an *umpire's instinct* for the game. For many umpires, the natural tendency is to watch the game as a fan rather than as an official. Constantly ask yourself questions about plays that might develop. If the shortstop throws the ball past the first baseman, does the umpire watch the ball as it bounces away, or does he head to second base to cover a possible play there? Does the umpire wait for the fielders to handle the ball before getting into position, or is he moving into position on the pitch? Does the umpire wait for a player to complain about a bad ball, or does he inspect the balls regularly? These are the things I look for when I evaulate the students at my umpire school.

Steady concentration

Like other forms of superior athletic performance, making good calls as an umpire requires more than good eyesight, good positioning, and good physical conditioning. It requires a level of concentration that athletes describe as an almost trancelike state of mind.

You have an advantage over the players in concentrating—you are not concerned about your batting average or how many games your team is out of first place. You can afford to be relaxed.

When you call a game, try to establish some kind of rhythm. I know of some athletes who always seem to be humming a tune or moving to some kind of regular beat. It's their way of approaching the game deliberately. Of course, some games are nothing but a set of disjointed actions. Errors, lags in the action, and wildness by the pitcher all break the game's rhythm. Whether or not the game flows smoothly on its own, you should try to establish some kind of inner rhythm.

One way to establish this rhythm is to constantly talk to yourself about the game. Remind yourself of the situation. If it helps, do a silent play-by-play of the game, with yourself as the star attraction. *Brinkman sets to watch the pitch, the ball veers toward the plate and catches the outside corner. Brinkman calls it a strike.* . . .

Jack Nicklaus, in his instructional manual for weekend golfers entitled *Golf My Way*, described the way he concentrates:

"I never hit a shot, even in practice, without having a very sharp, in-focus picture of it in my head. It's like a color movie. First, I 'see' the ball where I want it to finish, nice and white and sitting up on the bright green grass. Then the scene quickly changes and I 'see' the ball going there: its path, trajectory, and shape, even its behavior on landing. Then there's a sort of fade-out, and the next scene shows me making the kind of swing that will turn the previous images into reality."

The performances of other athletes are also evidence of the

Athletes and umpires have individual approaches to concentrating. Jack Nicklaus says he imagines a movie of his swing before every shot. My approach is to treat the game as a play-by-play announcer would. I try to anticipate what's going to happen next, and I picture the plays in my head. "Brinkman, the plate umpire, is responsible for making the tag calls at third base," I'll say to myself when I know my partners will have to cover other plays.

importance of the "inner game." These players go off into a cocoon, blocking out all activity outside their own performance. Rod Carew, of the California Angels, says he can visualize exactly where he can hit various pitches as they hurtle toward the plate. Steve Carlton, of the Philadelphia Phillies, always pitches as if he were alone with his catcher for an intense game of catch. When he was the St. Louis Cardinals' relief ace, Al Hrabosky used his "Mad Hungarian" act to achieve intense concentration.

The umpire must also achieve this intense level of concentration. The umpire won't *will* something to happen, like Jack Nicklaus. The umpire's job, after all, is to judge what others do, and he should not prejudge the play. But the umpire *can* anticipate watching players execute certain plays. How the umpire would call those plays would depend on whether the players deviate from that imaginary color movie. The plate umpire, for example, can imagine pitches moving into the strike zone. If the pitch does indeed move through the zone, it's a strike; otherwise, it's a ball.

The umpire should expect anything to happen on the field. But he should also anticipate what play will develop, like Jack Nicklaus and other great athletes do, and how he will rule when that play either goes according to or against the anticipated play.

Good judgment

Baseball is a game full of small but important idiosyncrasies.

A slight twitch in the pitcher's motion could signal a balk. An odd movement on the ball could signal an illegally thrown pitch. The split-second timing of a base runner's slide could indicate that the runner interfered with an infielder's attempt to complete a force play. A backlash of a batter's swing might be a sign that the batter was trying to interfere with the catcher.

To keep a game under control and within the confines of the rules, the umpire must be aware of these small movements.

Making judgment calls cannot be taught in a textbook. Good baseball judgment requires one part knowledge of rules, one part knowledge of human nature, and one part anticipation and preventive actions.

When the first baseman fields a ball with a man on, you must anticipate whether he will make a play at second or first base. When the batter hits a slicing liner to the outfield, you must decide whether or not you should cover the outfield. When the batter strolls to the dugout to wipe his bat, you must have an inkling of whether or not he's stalling. You must know where the ball is at all times so you won't get caught off guard on a hidden-ball trick or possible balk.

You must, in other words, be an observant student of baseball throughout every game.

Consistency

Nothing irks players and managers as much as an inconsistent umpire.

Different umpires have slightly different strike zones. Different umpires will look for different signs of balks. Different umpires will see a possible obstruction or interference call differently. Different umpires have different standards for the "phantom tag" (the second baseman or shortstop merely sweeps past, but does not tag, second base while turning a double play). Different umpires have different standards for players who barrel into second base trying to break up a double play. And they have different limits in their handling of arguments with players and managers.

There's not much the umpires can do about differences in judgment in cases like these, and the players and coaches usually understand that umpires have slightly different professional standards. But the teams need to know how far they can go. They will get understandably upset if the umpire applies different standards in similar situations.

If you're not sure if your call will be consistent with your partner's, talk to him about the play before the game or in between innings. If, for example, your partner allows the phantom tag during a double play, ask him about it. Then decide how you're going to call it—and if a coach asks you about it, tell him.

Everybody has bad days, when you just can't seem to get in a groove and see things right. How well you work when you're not up to snuff is the true indicator of your professionalism. Anyone can do a decent job if he's well rested and feeling good. It takes a certain amount of professionalism, though, to stick with a game and force yourself to concentrate.

Once you start calling a game, treat each pitch and each play as if it were the last call you will ever make. If you think you might have made a mistake, don't think about it on subsequent calls. Just leave the mistake behind and call the rest of the game.

Objectivity

The most serious affront to an umpire's professionalism is the charge that he favors one team over another. You must not allow yourself to be liable for this charge.

In *The Essence of the Game Is Deception*, Leonard Koppett's book about basketball strategy and folkways, he contends that the reason professional basketball teams enjoy a home-court advantage is the referees. Koppett argues that officiating basketball games is an impossible task and that a referee cannot hope to make nearly as many accurate calls as officials of other sports. When the referee is working in an arena with 15,000 constantly screaming fanatics, he cannot help but be subtly influenced to give close calls to the home team.

Koppett, a sportswriter for *The New York Times*, cites an impressive array of statistics to support his claims. I am not sure if his thesis is correct, but I do know that it cannot be correct for baseball.

Umpiring baseball games is at once the easiest and most difficult of all sports. Although baseball has its share of continuous plays, the bulk of the game is waiting for plays to happen and getting into position to see them happen. Unlike basketball or football, where the referees must keep an eye on several activities at a time while moving up and down the field or court, umpires usually just need to intently watch one play at a time.

That makes the job manageable. It also means the umpire will be held accountable for his rulings. Everyone in the ballpark watches what the umpire does. He is under constant scrutiny.

Earl Weaver, the manager of the Baltimore Orioles, used to say certain teams "owned" certain umpires. When umpire Bill Haller's brother Tom played for the Detroit Tigers, Weaver made a stink about the possibility that Bill's calls would favor his brother. It was hogwash, but Weaver made enough noise to keep Bill away from Tigers–Orioles games. If blood relations had anything to do with competitiveness in sports, why would brothers be so competitive against each other as players? I can't think of a tougher pitching duel than Phil Niekro versus Joe Niekro.

Baseball is a game of conditioned reflexes. When you're working a game, you usually don't have more than a split second to consider each call. That's not enough time to let your feelings enter into your decision-making if you vow to start each pitch with a fresh mind. It's almost impossible *not* to be an objective umpire.

The key to remaining objective in baseball is not ignoring the rabid fans, like it is in basketball, but in starting over with each new play. Once you start thinking about past calls when you are making new calls, you will lose your consistency—and objectivity.

Knowledge of the rules

Section 9.01(c) is the umpire's favorite part of the Official Baseball Rules. That is the section that gives the umpire the final authority over "any point not specifically covered in these rules." Just as the 10th Amendment to the U.S. Constitution reserves all undelegated authority to the states, this section reserves all authority for undefined situations to the umpires.

9.00—The Umpire

9.01 (a) The league president shall appoint one or more umpires to officiate at each league championship game. The umpires shall be responsible for the conduct of the game in accordance with these official rules and for maintaining discipline and order on the playing field during the game.

(b) Each umpire is the representative of the league and of professional baseball, and is authorized and required to enforce all of these rules. Each umpire has authority to order a player, coach, manager or club officer or employee to do or refrain from doing anything which affects the administering of these rules, and to enforce the prescribed penalties.

(c) Each umpire has authority to rule on any point not specifically covered in these rules.

(d) Each umpire has authority to disqualify any player, coach, manager or substitute for objecting to decisions or for unsportsmanlike conduct or language, and to eject such disqualified person from the playing field. If an umpire disqualifies a player while a play is in progress, the disqualification shall not take effect until no further action is possible in that play.

(e) Each umpire has authority at his discretion to eject from the playing field (1) any person whose duties permit his presence on the field, such as ground crew members, ushers, photographers, newsmen, broadcasting crew members, etc., and (2) any spectator or other person not authorized to be on the playing field.

Here is the umpire's favorite section of the rulebook. Make sure you also know the other, more specific rules.

Fortunately, this favorite rule rarely needs to be invoked. The rulebook covers almost every conceivable situation that could develop on the playing field.

It is your job as an umpire to know all the rules, and to know how to use the rulebook. Situations could develop in which you would need to refer quickly to the rulebook during a game, so you should know exactly where to turn to settle a dispute.

Whenever you get a chance, study the rulebook. Try to imagine plays that could develop in a game for each rule. And when you're involved in a play that involves a sticky rule interpretation, make a note of the incident by the rule in question in your rulebook.

Good relations with the teams

The two teams in any game need the cooperation of the umpires in order for a game to proceed smoothly. The umpires need the cooperation of both teams' members. It is in the interests of both the umpires and the members of the teams to establish a good working relationship.

Umpires should be friendly to the members of both teams, and they should try to work with the players to assure them the best-called game possible. The umpires should be willing to explain their calls and any rule questions that arise during a game, but they should avoid being drawn into protracted discussions about hypothetical situations.

There is no "right" way of dealing with players. Some umpires are more talkative than others. Some exchange pleasantries with the players—they talk idly about restaurants and movies and the state of the world. There's nothing wrong with that as long as it doesn't develop into a situation where the player thinks he has your friendship. Don't become buddies with the players.

I am generally pretty quiet on the field. I figure my job is to stay on top of the game and make the calls—not serve as a socialite—on the field. But it's OK to talk with players as long as you don't get involved in discussions of hypothetical situations. The players will remember what you tell them and, in the middle of an argument, try to use the old "But you told me last inning . . ." routine. That can develop into long-lasting troubles.

Avoid talking with fans. Once the fans think of you as some-

Chances are you'll work with the players and coaches on both
teams several games a year—and several seasons in a row. It's
in your best interest to have good relations with the teams. That
doesn't mean you have to become best buddies with the players,
but you should develop a good working relationship.

thing other than an impartial observer, they'll start taunting you
from the stands. They'll think they know you and can influence
you. It's just not worth the bother.

Once the game is over, leave the field right away. Your job's
over.

A word on being human

Umpires (gasp) sometimes make mistakes. What separates
the good umpires from the bad is not only how many mistakes
they make, but also how they behave after they goof.

When Ron Luciano—now a best-selling author and a star in
a Hollywood movie about baseball—first came to the major leagues
he startled managers and players by candidly admitting his mistakes. He would call a player out at second base on an attempted
steal, the players and managers would jump up and down and
scream in his face, and Ron would say something like, "Gee, I blew
that one. We umpires are only human too, you know." For a while,

such honesty and humility stifled the players. What else could they do? The ump was on their side, but he couldn't change his call and everybody knew it.

After a while, however, his candor started to irritate the teams more than it placated them, and that hurt Ron's effectiveness as an umpire. Ron would admit kicking a call, and the managers and players would rage. "Why in the name of Kennesaw Mountain Landis," they would steam, "is an umpire who *admits* screwing up in the major leagues?"

In the annual assessment of umpires by the American League's general managers, Ron Luciano was rated the league's best umpire in 1977. The next year, he was rated the worst by the same general managers. Ron was the same umpire, but his honesty was upsetting to the G.M.s. And as we've said before, having the respect and cooperation of the teams is essential to good umpiring.

Yes, all umpires make mistakes. What should you do if you boot a call as an umpire? Maybe remind yourself to concentrate, and be patient with the manager and players who argue the play, but otherwise do your job as you always have. Whatever you do, don't make a habit of telling the players you made a mistake.

Umpires make mistakes when they are out of position or do not concentrate on the play. If you think you made a mistake, silently scold yourself. "You dummy! You kicked that play because, while you *looked* at the play, you didn't really pay attention to what was happening and when it was happening."

If you get an argument from the team that was victimized by your mistake, be a little more patient than usual. Hear them out. Most coaches and players realize you can't change your decision; you'd get an even angrier reaction from the other team and the game would take forever to finish. They'll simmer down if you listen calmly.

On occasion, you might be best off admitting that you *might* have missed the play. Every umpire, including yours truly, has called the most obvious strike a ball. You make so many calls over the course of a game that mistakes are inevitable. You might say: "Look, Skip, maybe I messed up, but I can't change the call so let's get back to playing ball."

Only admit the most obvious mistakes, and don't make a show of your contrition. There have been times when I thought I missed a play, but when the eleven o'clock news came on that night I saw that I actually got the play right. Umpiring is a job of conditioned reflexes. There will be many times when your immediate response will be more accurate than your mental instant-replays or the partial analysis of angry players.

The umpire can step into two traps after he thinks he has missed a call. The first trap is to want to "even the score" with the victimized team by giving the team the benefit of the doubt on the next close play. The second trap is a desire to be consistent, even when you're wrong; if you called a ball just outside the strike zone a strike, for example, you'd call all subsequent pitches in the same spot strikes just to show the players how consistent you are.

If you fall into either trap, you'll be distracted the whole game. You'll be keeping score in your head: "Hmmmm, I owe the Dodgers a close call with men in scoring position. . . ." Or: "If there's any doubt on a tag-up play, I'll give it to the Yankees because they got hurt by my call last time." This kind of thinking will drive you crazy, and you'll make more mistakes. You will also bring on a hail of taunts from both benches.

A country-western song says: "Some days are diamonds. Some days are stones." You're going to have your share of rough days when you just don't have much concentration or interest in the game. That's true for everyone—ballplayer, umpire, fan. People understand that. Don't try to compensate by "evening the score." Compensate by bearing down.

THREE
The Umpire's Routine

The best people in any given profession are those who can't bring themselves to punch a time clock—the ones who just can't stand to live the drab "day in the life" that the Beatles sang about.

A good newspaper reporter, for example, thinks about his beat in his spare time as well as in the newsroom. He picks up tips at barbeques and softball games as well as in the office. A good judge does not think about the law exclusively within the confines of the courtroom. In his private life, he is a student of society and political philosophy. A good architect thinks about the principles of his work—the aesthetic beauty of a structure, the physical problems of construction—not only as he sits before a drafting table but also as he looks at buildings on a leisurely walk.

So it is with umpiring. You can't hope to do a professional job of officiating a baseball game without interesting yourself in more than the routine decision-making of a ball game. To be an excellent umpire, you must constantly think about baseball. You must make sure that your physical condition allows you to move around on the field. You should approach baseball like a student of the game, as most players are, and be prepared for any situation that might develop when you are on the field.

Know the game

Branch Rickey, the longtime general manager of the Brooklyn Dodgers, once said that "luck is the residue of design." When someone is in the right place at the right time, it's probably because that person prepared himself for that situation beforehand. Likewise, the work of a good umpire begins before he's assigned to work a game.

The most important ways to improve your umpiring are to watch a lot of baseball games and to join an umpires' association. Baseball is a relatively simple game, but the slowness and predictability of many games can also explode into difficult situations.

Watch as many baseball games as you can, not just major-league games on television, but local high-school and semi-professional games as well. Try to see as many games as possible of the league in which you will be working. When you watch those games, try to watch the *umpires' game*—don't always focus your attention on the contest between the two teams. Consider yourself the director of umpire development in the league, and pretend that you're there to evaluate the umpires who are working the game.

Especially at the beginning of your career as an umpire, try to evaluate the umpires formally. Bring a pad and pencil, and take notes. Ask yourself questions such as:

How do the umpires look? Do they look like a professional team, or do they look like a ragtag outfit? Do they take command without appearing to be too bossy? In short, do they have a good attitude?

How are the umpires' voices and signals? Do they make their calls clear to everyone in the ballpark? Do the umpires appear to believe in their own calls? Do they have good timing, or do they make calls too quickly or too slowly? Do they sell their calls the right way?

Do the umpires hustle? Do they get in good position to make calls? Do they look alert or lazy? Do they beat the ball to the play? Are they ready to watch a play before it happens? Do they look like they know where they're going as a play unfolds? Do they stay out of the players' way during plays?

Do the umpires communicate well with each other? Do they communicate with hand signals or by calling out reminders and advice to each other? Are those signals understandable to everyone in the park or just the umpires?

How do the umpires deal with any disputes that develop? Are they in command of the rules? Do they command the respect of the coaches and players?

Your "spring training"

Especially at the beginning of the year, umpires should consider working practice games as part of their own training. Like the players, umpires get out of shape and lose their competitive edge during the off-season.

You also might want to work on a specific part of your technique during practice games. Officials in the American League office told me one spring that I looked a little too nonchalant behind the plate. Until that spring, I had gotten down on one knee to make the ball-strike calls. The league officials said that technique made me look too relaxed—and some coaches and players were disturbed because I wasn't as tensed up and aggressive as they were. So I worked all spring on the traditional crouch.

Without special projects like that, it usually takes me four or five exhibition games in the Grapefruit League to get physically ready for the season. It's good to work in even more practice games so you can refresh your knowledge of rules and game situations.

The amount of help and comradeship that umpires can get from other umpires varies a great deal from group to group. Most umpire associations hold regular meetings for their officials. Those umpires can discuss rules and plays that develop over the course of a season. Some groups offer clinics where experienced as well as inexperienced umpires get help on their mechanics. Some associations send their officials to games to watch the performance of the umpires—and then they talk to those umpires about their strengths and weaknesses.

Baseball has the worst record of all professional sports when it comes to evaluating and helping its working umpires. Major-league umpires are the only pro-sports officials who don't have annual clinics where the officials receive the scrutiny and advice of the people in charge. For some reason, baseball just hasn't seen the virtue of professionals working together to stay sharp.

Equipment check

Before you leave the house for a game, you should take an equipment inventory. Start from your feet and work up to your head as you check to see that you have the equipment you need to work the game.

You will need the following pieces of equipment to work a baseball game:

* *Footwear.* More than anyone else involved in the game, you're going to be doing a lot of standing and running. Your feet are going to hurt if you don't get the right kind of socks and shoes to work a game.

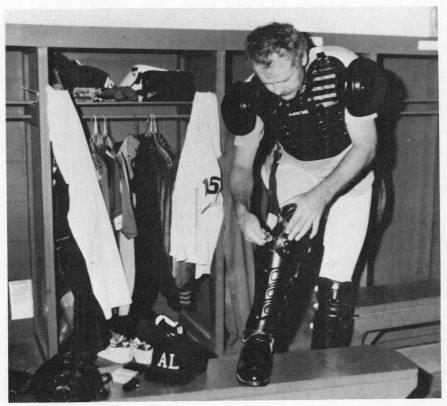

Before each game, make a thorough check of your umpiring clothing and gear. Start from your feet and slowly work up to your head.

Get shoes with a hard sole with deep cushions to absorb the shocks of running and pivoting, and made of durable material. Make sure the shoe has a good arch. Also make sure it fits well: a poor fit will negate otherwise good construction. If you are working behind the plate, get a pair of shoes with a protective steel toe. Nothing hurts more than a ball that is fouled down on your feet. And, believe me, nobody will have sympathy for you when you're hopping around in pain after a hard foul.

Many companies make black, studded athletic shoes for use on the bases. Currently, the major-league umpires are wearing Puma shoes.

Get a couple pairs of white all-cotton or all-wool socks to wear underneath some black or dark blue socks during the game. The white socks should keep your feet cool.

- *Long johns and a jock and cup.* A pair of thin, all-cotton long johns will absorb sweat throughout the game and keep it from running down your legs. If it's a hot day and you sweat a lot, the dampness of the long johns will keep you cool. The long johns will also protect your pants from rotting away because of the sweat.

- *Chest protector.* Most baseball leagues have made an important change in chest protectors in recent years. The traditional "balloon" protector has been replaced by the more flexible "inside" protector. The balloon protector is a slab of foam rubber covered with dark blue material that the umpire holds in front of himself during pitches. The inside protector is simply a catcher's chest protector with shoulder pads.

  We'll discuss the two kinds of protectors in more detail in Chapter 5.

- *Uniform and a change of shirts.* Most associations have standards for umpires' clothing. Most ask the umpire to wear dark blue or gray pants, a light blue shirt with a collar, and a dark blue cap. Home plate umpires' caps should have a slightly shorter bill so the umpire's mask can fit over the cap easily.

- *Mask.* Several kinds of masks for both umpires and catchers are now available in most sporting goods stores. Most umpires and catchers today use masks with an elaborate wire front rather than masks with a few thick horizontal bars. The wire masks allow greater peripheral vision. A few major-league umpires and catchers—notably catcher Bob Boone of the Cali-

Today's mask allows the umpire greater peripheral vision than the old heavy-bar masks.

fornia Angels—still use the bar-type masks.

Whatever you choose, make sure you can put the mask snugly on your head and quickly take it off. Some umpires wear a protective "tongue" that hangs from the bottom of the mask; it protects the throat from a foul ball or missed pitch.

Before every game, check the mask for defects—a crack in the frame, a loosened wire welding—that would endanger you during the game. Masks are made pretty strong these days, but a quick check can't hurt.

Practice taking off the mask with your left hand a few times before each game. You need to use your left hand to remove the mask but your left hand will also hold the ball-strike indicator. Use your right hand to make the safe-out, fair-foul, or catch-no-catch calls.

• *Rulebook.* There's nothing wrong with bringing a rulebook to a game. Referring to a rulebook on the field is not a sign of weakness. It's kind of inconvenient to carry—it gets dirty and sweaty if it's in your hip pocket. So just keep it near your bags by the field. It shouldn't be needed that often, but it's good to have on hand. You shouldn't be ashamed to refer to it in a pinch.

Baseball's rules cover just about any conceivable situation that could develop on the field, but there are so many rules that situations are bound to develop in which nobody really knows for sure what the rules say. There will be times when the two teams and the umpires will disagree about whether, say, a batter who hits out of turn can score a run. It's always bad when you have to take a rules dispute to the league with a formal protest. You're always better off resolving a rule dispute on the field.

- *Indicator.* The home plate umpire should always carry an indicator. I would advise that the base umpire carry one also, especially in a ballpark without a scoreboard. The indicator is a small device used to keep track of the balls, strikes, and outs in each inning. Silly as it sounds, using the indicator requires a little practice. It takes a certain amount of dexterity to flip the right dial on the indicator.

- *Brush.* The plate umpire needs a small brush to clean off home plate. I suggest that this be done during the natural pauses in the action.

Here's the ball-strike-out indicator. Coordinating your fingers to record the count can be a little tricky.

On the way to the game . . .

The advisability of eating and drinking before and during a game varies from umpire to umpire. It also varies according to the weather.

Most umpires and athletes eat lightly before games. The old-time umpire school instructors used to tell us to avoid eating or drinking anything during games because it looked "unprofessional." But as long as you don't eat more food than you can digest in, say, an hour, you'll be OK.

Don't drink alcohol before the game. You've probably seen videotapes of driving tests involving people who have had one or two drinks. These people have a hard time driving between cones on the road at minimal speeds. Well, baseball can be a high-speed game. You can't expect to be quick enough to make all the decisions if you have Miller Time in your blood.

The sun dehydrates the body, and you've got to replenish the liquid supplies. Bring water, iced tea, or Gatorade to the game.

For the umpire, going to a baseball game is a lot like going to a party where you know there will be a lot of unfamiliar faces. There is a tendency to get tense. You must brace yourself for a series of awkward situations with players. You have to be calm and confident when you reach the ballpark. Racing fans say they bet against a horse that sweats before the day's races. That horse is just too worn out to be any good. The same goes for umpires. Avoid too much activity before games.

The more you know about a game's conditions, the better you'll handle the stress. One very important game condition is the man you'll be working with. Get to know your umpiring partner as much as possible before the game.

If possible, drive to the game with your partner. Get to know something about your partner's experience and approach to umpiring. Not all umpires have the same approach to a game—nor should they. Some umpires like to cover plays that develop on the bases in different ways. For example, some umpire crews will have the plate umpire cover a play at third base, while others will have the field umpire cover that play. Different umpiring crews also have different systems for covering the fair-foul and catch-no-catch plays in the outfield.

All this advice, of course, underscores the importance of having a system. Why make an educated guess that your umpiring partner will cover a play when you can be certain with a system? If you use an ad hoc system—"I'll cover third if I can get there, otherwise you take it"—you'll get 95 percent of the plays. Those plays will practically call themselves. But the other 5 percent will give you a tough time.

Many umpires work well because they instinctively know whether they or their partners should cover a play. But it's better to work out a formal system, especially if you have not worked with the other umpire before.

Your partner is the only ally you have on the field. Make sure you both understand each other and are prepared to back each other up throughout the game. Knowing and working well with your partner will not only help you know what to expect during the game, but it will also impress the two teams' players and managers. They will know you are a team, and they will know that they can't play you off each other.

When you're on the way to the game, discuss the field's ground rules, how the weather and field conditions are likely to affect the game, and how you plan to communicate with each other. If you know something about the teams, talk about that, too. Do the teams try to steal a lot of bases?

Also talk about your plans for asking for help on the field. If the defensive team questions whether the batter checks a swing, should the umpire ask his partner in the field? How are you going to deal with a sticky rule situation?

Ask your partner to be frank in his assessment of your performance. Every once in a while, you will make a call that the players and coaches protest. You might be a little uncertain (especially after all the hollering) about whether you made the right call. If you can turn to your partner for a straight (and private) opinion of your performance, you'll be a better, more alert umpire. Tell your partner that you want his *honest* opinion—ask him not to just tell you what he thinks you want to hear.

Limbering up

Umpires do not have to be able to perform half as many physical feats as the players. But all umpires should be in decent shape, and they should loosen up before every game by doing stretching exercises. Short sprints and quick pivots prepare you better for a game than long, loping runs. Your movement during games is going to be short and quick.

When you do these exercises, avoid bouncing or jerking actions. The idea behind stretching is to pull those muscles out like rubber bands so they're nimble during the game. Jerking actions will not help you stretch the muscles and they could hurt you. Also, don't get too ambitious with your stretching. If you over-stretch, you could damage the muscles' connective tissues. Follow the stretching exercises with a "cooling off" period, when you can relax.

Here are some stretching exercises I suggest:

- *Trunk twist*. Stand erect with your arms straight out to each side at shoulder height. Twist right, then left, about twenty times. Go faster as you progress.
- *Floor touch*. Stand erect with your feet about two feet apart. Bend forward with your knees straight, and touch the floor. Go easy the first two or three times, then speed up the exercise until you've done it about fifteen times.
- *Hamstring stretch*. Stand erect, placing your left heel on the seat of a chair. Keeping both legs straight, bend forward until you feel some pressure on the hamstring, which is the muscle in the back of the upper leg. Stretch it slowly. Raise the height until you can do this exercise on a tabletop instead of on the seat of a chair. Do the same for the right leg. Do ten to fifteen with each leg.

Get limbered up before each game. Baseball isn't the most physically taxing sport, but it does have bursts of action that require the players and umpires to be in shape. If you don't loosen up before a game, you could find yourself twisting a knee or pulling a hamstring when you move on a routine play. These diagrams show a few of the pregame exercises most umpires use.

- *Toe touch*. Do the same thing as with the floor touch, this time touching your feet with opposite hands.
- *Achilles tendon drill*. Place a bat or a large book on the floor. Stand with the front of your feet touching the object. With

Trunk Twist

Hamstring Stretch

Floor and Toe Touch

Achilles Tendon Drill

Deep Knee Bends

your legs stiff and heels touching the floor, lean forward. Try to touch the bat or book. Do this exercise slowly. Do it until the backs of your legs are fully stretched.

• *Deep knee bends.* Stand erect with your feet a couple feet apart and your weight distributed evenly. Take a deep breath and exhale as you squat down into a catcher's position. Do this five to seven times, slowly, and you'll be OK.

Check field conditions

When you arrive at the ballpark, walk around the infield and outfield to get a feel for the field conditions. Knowing the playing conditions not only prepares you for setting ground rules at the pregame meeting at home plate, but it also enables you to anticipate what will happen on the field during some plays.

How is the wind going to affect the game? Is the infield grass high or low? Is the field wet or dry? Smooth or rocky? Does the outfield fence pose any problems—for example, a hole, or weak supports that would cause the fence to collapse if a fielder hit it? Are the foul lines clearly marked? If not, are there some marks in the field that you can use as demarcations for foul balls? Does the seating of the spectators present the possibility of interference? Is there a bat rack or other equipment on the field that could get in the way of the players?

The Delaware River ritual

Before each game, the home plate umpire should get the game's baseballs from the home team and then go to work rubbing them up for the games.

Because baseballs *look* best when they are nice and shiny and spanking clean, baseball manufacturers sell the balls with a gloss that makes gripping the ball difficult for pitchers and fielders. The plate umpire should smack a little dab of mud on the balls and rub them up to make handling them easier.

The major leagues get all the mud they use to rub up balls from the bottom of the Delaware River. The leagues send coffee cans of the stuff to all big-league ballparks, who in turn pass it on to the umpires. Mud from the Delaware is said to have the best consistency of any mud for baseballs. I'm sure mud from the bottom of the puddle in the ballpark's parking lot will do just as well.

The meeting at home plate

As soon as you arrive at the park, check in with the managers or coaches for both teams. They should know that you are ready to start the game on time and that any delay in the game is the fault of the teams, not the umpires.

Before each game, the umpires must meet with representatives of both teams at home plate. Collect the lineup cards from each team, and give each team a copy of the other team's card. Ask the managers to list their reserve players, with the players' numbers, on the back of the lineup cards. If both teams accept each other's roster, you'll avoid arguments about whether or not certain players are eligible to play.

Go over the ground rules that are peculiar to the ballpark. Let the home team's manager set the tempo of the ground rules discussion. If there is a dispute about a ground rule, the plate umpire will make the final decision.

Don't let the managers lure you into a discussion of what kind of umpire you are. Don't tell them, "Well, I call a low strike." But you should allow the managers to tell you something about the idiosyncratic moves of their players, especially their pitchers and base runners.

*A familiar sight for any baseball fan is the pregame meeting
between umpires and managers. Especially when one of the
umpires or teams is working in the ballpark for the first time,
it's important that the umpires discuss all of the park's possible
idiosyncrasies. An ounce of prevention. . . .*

Expect the unexpected

When you finally get into position for the first pitch of the
game, try to think of all the plays that might develop in the game.
Base runners and fielders sometimes behave in unpredictable
ways. Anticipate all the ways a player can react to a situation so
you don't get caught off guard.

I can think of quite a few times when I was leaning the wrong
way on plays because I didn't anticipate what the players were

going to do. Usually, those plays involved exceptional fielders who, because of their skill, were able to go after the important out instead of the sure out. In amateur leagues, the unpredictability is more likely the result of a player's not knowing which way to go with a play.

I was working the plate one day in Kansas City. The Royals were in the field against the Toronto Blue Jays. The Jays had a man on third with two outs when Lloyd Moseby hit a shot to third base. Most third basemen would go to first base for the sure out, but the Royals' George Brett thought he had a tough play at first and instead threw home. The ball almost beaned me, I was so surprised. I recovered just in time to see the bang-bang play at the plate.

The same kind of thing happened with first baseman Eddie Murray of the Baltimore Orioles, this time on a "swinging bunt" down the first-base line. Murray realized the play at first would be close, so he threw to home. The play even surprised the O's catcher, Rick Dempsey.

If you have looked over the field, studied the teams' lineups, and if you stay aware of game situations, you should be prepared for any play.

Winding down

Just as preparing for a game requires a great deal of energy, so does recovering from the stresses of the game—especially when you're involved in a controversial decision on the field.

During my early years as an umpire, I got too involved in the day's activities. If a manager gave me a hard time or the league office failed to back me up, I would steam for hours after the game. I let the day's events control me long after I left the park.

Dealing with the pressures of umpiring can be tough. After our pine tar ruling in 1983, umpire Tim McClelland ran into a bunch of Royals at an airport. He got nothing but sneers and icy stares from them, as if to say, *You, McClelland, were out to get us. What do you have against us, anyway? That call you made has killed whatever civility we may have had for you.* It was tough on Tim, a rookie umpire who thought he would at least get the respect he deserved for doing his best.

Over the years, I have learned to understand that the players and fans do not mean to direct their emotions at me personally but rather at my role as umpire. They usually just don't *think* when they make an insult. Probably because I have talked with hundreds of other umpires who have gone through the same ordeal, I now have the discipline to ignore the immature sniping from players and fans.

When you finish a tough game, the temptation is to immediately take your sweaty body to the closest bar for a couple of beers, a pizza, and a rehash of the latest game. Try to be a little more imaginative in devising a postgame routine.

After a day of changing bedpans and taking orders from doctors, a nurse will take a long shower and change into pedestrian clothes. After a day of analyzing legal briefs, an attorney will play handball or start a barbeque. After an early day of deliveries, a truck driver will take in a matinee movie.

All of these people are, deliberately, removing themselves from the stresses of their work. As Lady Macbeth tried to do in her hand-washing scene, they try to cleanse their psyches of the day's troubles.

You, too, should cleanse your system of the day's stresses. After a game, get away from the park right away. Take a shower. Listen to some music. Eat some good food. After you relax, go over any mechanics or rules mistakes you made. Make a record of them so you won't make the same mistake twice. This will make you a better umpire.

FOUR
Making the Calls

The scene belongs in a Broadway musical like *Damn Yankees*.

The top students from professional baseball's two umpire schools, wearing assorted combinations of sweatsuits, gym shorts, and tee shirts, are lined up in four or five rows with six young men in each row. They stand with their hands on their knees. An older man, wearing a windbreaker, breaks the early morning stillness with a series of commands.

First, the older man shouts: "Go!" The young men break from their hands-on-knees position and start running. The older man orders them to stop, and they stop. The young men then return to their hands-on-knees position. The older man tells the students to "call it," and the young men extend their right hands to the front of their bodies and jerk their fists back, shouting, "He's out!"

The drill sergeant continues barking orders for about fifteen minutes. The young men run back and forth between right field and left field, polishing their technique for calling runners safe and out, balls foul and fair, attempted catches successful and unsuccessful. They finally gather around the man wearing the windbreaker, an official with the umpire development branch of the National Association of Professional Baseball.

"Now, we've been teaching you how to make these calls one way so we could judge you all fairly," says Barney Deary, director of umpire development for the association. "But there's not only one right way to make a call. You should now also develop your own style. For example, on a called third strike, some plate umpires like to pull the chain to sell the call." Deary shows the technique, where the plate umpire turns to his right and imitates someone pulling the chain of a power saw or hedge clipper. "That's dramatic," he says. "That sells your call."

The scene is the five-diamond complex in Bradenton, Florida, called Pirate City. The two dozen rookie professional umpires are attending a week-long "finishing school" to hone their umpiring skills before the start of their first spring training games.

Fans often make fun of the way professional umpires make their calls. The styles of the umpires are all distinct. Some chirp their calls out quickly. Others make their calls last a while: "Strahhhhhhhhhhhhiiiiiiiiiii*ike*!" Others dance around, almost executing a full pirouette, spinning 180 degrees on one foot before shooting the right arm in the air and barking: *"Out!"* Ron Luciano had the most amusing acts. When he called base runners out, he pretended to shoot them with an imaginary pistol. "Bang! Bang!" he said as he pointed his finger at the frustrated runner.

Many professional umpires do indeed look silly on the field when they make their calls. But, believe it or not, reasons exist for those umpires to go into such complicated physical gyrations and make such strange noises.

In one way or another, the drama of the calls helps the umpire to tell everyone in the ballpark exactly what's going on all the time, and it also tells everyone that the umpires are paying attention and are in complete control of the game. Making loud calls on plays, and making clear, understandable signals that everyone in the ballpark can see and understand, are the umpire's main ways of controlling the tempo of the game.

It's important for everyone in the ballpark to understand the umpire's signals. Making an out or safe call is pretty easy, but you'd be surprised how few umpires make the calls so that everyone can understand them.

At the Joe Brinkman Umpire School, we videotape the students making calls. The students are constantly amazed to learn that they don't always make good, crisp calls. They realize only after seeing themselves on the tube that they didn't jerk their fist all the way on an out call or that they didn't make their infield fly rule call loud enough for everyone to hear. After the videotape sessions, the students get right to work to improve their signals.

Of course, not everybody has access to videotaping equipment or has the critical eye of Barney Deary. To work on your calls, stand in front of a large mirror and make all the calls several times. Have someone shout out calls for you to make, and make them right in front of that mirror. Tell your helper to mix up the calls so that there's an element of surprise. Umpires make their weakest calls when they're moving and don't know what to expect. Simulate these situations as much as possible.

Getting into position

There are two ways to get ready to watch a play happen—the set position and the standing set position.

In the set position, the umpire stands with his hands on his knees. The feet should be spread out at least as wide as your shoulders, with the knees comfortably bent. Put your right foot slightly back, with your toes even with your left instep.

In the standing set position, you are not hunched over quite as much. Keep your hands at your sides, and keep your knees slightly flexed.

The key to using both positions is to make a complete stop so you can watch the play without moving. If you're moving, you're going to be distracted when the play is happening. Don't even move your head when the play is happening. Let your eyes do the moving. If you have the proper angle to see the play, you shouldn't have to move your head.

Making the calls

The safe and out calls. To make the safe call from the set position, raise your hands in front of your body at shoulder height. Quickly move your hands from the front of your body to your sides. At the same time you're moving your hands, bark out: "Safe!"

To make the out call from the same position, extend your right hand as if you were about to shake someone's hand. Make a fist with the hand. Jerk that hand up quickly, with your arm extended, and shout: "He's out!"

It's important to extend your arms when making the safe and out calls, as well as most other calls. This exaggerated motion gives everyone in the ballpark a good view of what you're doing. If you

Safe.

Out.

lift your arm without extending it when you're making an out call, the call will be hard for many people to see—especially for those on the side of the diamond opposite to the umpire's arms.

Fair ball, foul ball. The most important thing to remember about making the fair-foul call is to be absolutely still when you watch the play. Get in the standing set position, straddling the foul line, to watch the play. You'll never be able to see clearly whether the ball goes fair or foul unless you are on the line.

If the ball is fair, step in and point to the ball with the arm closest to the playing field. Your wrist should be slightly above the elbow. Do not speak when you make this call.

When the ball is foul, straddle the line and raise your hands over your head as if you were making a time-out or touchdown signal in football. Then point to foul territory right away. If the ball was very close to the line, you'll probably want to make the call more emphatically, so throw both arms toward foul territory. A little body English goes a long way in selling close calls.

You should not make a verbal call on fair balls, but always shout "Foul" when the ball is foul. The players and coaches involved in the play must know whether or not they have to keep running or chasing the ball, and they need to get back to their original positions if the ball is foul.

Strike, foul tip, ball. The signal for the strike is similar to the signal for the out. The plate umpire, however, should consider a few things while making the strike call that he doesn't think about when making the out call.

Because there are so many pitches in a game, the plate umpire would be silly to go through the full routine when he makes most strike calls. Most strike calls occur when the batter swings and misses or looks at a pitch that obviously cuts through the strike zone. There's no need to be dramatic when you call those pitches strikes. Simply jerking your right fist or punching the air is enough to tell everyone in the ballpark that you have recorded the obvious strike.

Save your dramatic motion for called third strikes and the close pitches—the pitches where you have to convince the players, coaches, and fans that you saw it right. If a pitcher just hits the inside corner with a pitch, be dramatic. If a batter tries to check his swing but you decide he went around, be dramatic. Use the

Fair.

Foul.

chainsaw strike that Deary demonstrated. These close calls are the ones you have to sell to the participants.

If the batter hits a foul tip, turn to one side, put your left arm up with a fist, while your right arm slides across the wrist and fist, and then indicate with the fingers the number of the strike.

If a pitch is a ball, simply bark a clear, crisp "Ball!" if it's close. Otherwise, quietly state your call. If the pitch is the fourth ball on the batter, you might want to make your call louder, "Ball four!" and say "Take your base." This is especially true in youth leagues, because the kids don't always know when to leave the box.

Catch or no-catch.   The catch or no-catch call usually develops on balls that are hit softly to the shallow part of the outfield and on balls that are hit hard but just barely within the grasp of the running fielder. That is one of the most exciting plays and one of the most difficult calls to make.

Get ready to watch the play in the standing set position. When the fielder catches the ball, make the normal out call and yell: "He's out!" When the fielder misses the ball, wave your arms in the safe motion and yell: "No catch!"

Most balls do not require a fair-foul or catch-no-catch call. After most situations, there is no need to go into the outfield to cover the ball. Get in your regular position unless it looks like there's going to be a close call one way or another.

On balls where you have to make both a fair-foul call and a catch-no-catch call, make the fair-foul call first.

Infield fly rule.   All umpires on the field should make this call at about the same time. Because this is something of an oddball play, the umpires should tell the players and coaches promptly what's going on. They should know if the umpires are invoking the rule when the pop fly has reached the top of its arc and is about to fall to the ground.

If any one umpire invokes the infield fly rule, then that is the call, even if the other umpire does not think the call should have been made. That way there is no danger of umpires crossing up the players by making conflicting calls.

To call the infield fly, point into the air with your right arm. Shout: "Infield fly! Batter is out!" If it looks like the ball could go either fair or foul, shout: "Infield fly! If fair!"

Interference and obstruction.   The umpire must bear in mind sever-

Infield fly call.

Spectator interference.

al things when an interference or obstruction play develops.

Some interference plays will make the ball dead right away; others will make the ball dead only after the play has been completed. Depending on the situation, call time out at the appropriate time. Then tell the players, in short phrases, what happened and what remedies you are prescribing as umpire. "Time! Interference!" The runner bumped the fielder as he tried to field the ground ball! The runner is out!"

Obstruction occurs when a defensive player who is not making a play touches a base runner. When that happens, point to the offending fielder, and shout: "That's obstruction!" Let the players complete the play, then impose the appropriate penalties.

Dead ball, time out, play ball.   Umpires declare the ball to be dead in two ways: immediately, and on a delayed basis. When the ball should be called dead right away—for example, when the batter is hit by a pitch—the umpire should raise his arms straight up and shout: "The ball is dead." If the play involves a delayed dead ball situation such as catcher's interference, hold your left fist straight out to the side and allow the players to complete the play.

To call time out, simply raise your arms high in the air. To make the ball live again and resume play, order the pitcher to step on the rubber with the ball and get ready to pitch, then motion to the pitcher with the right hand and say: "Play ball!"

Balk and other awards of bases.   When a pitcher commits a balk, point to the pitcher and shout "Balk!" Then tell the base runners that they may advance to the next base. When you're awarding the batter or base runners a base, point toward the base and say something like: "You! Take third base on the balk!"

When you make a balk call, try to be quick enough so the pitcher doesn't actually release the ball. The pitcher is liable for throwing the ball away. He should know when he commits the balk right away so he doesn't compound his problems with an errant throw.

Selling calls

A new term is gaining acceptance in legal circles. It's "proportionality." The umpire should be familiar with the term when he makes calls on the field. In umpiring, "proportionality" means fitting the call with the importance and closeness of the play.

If the batter hits a hard ground ball to the second baseman, and the second baseman's throw to first base easily beats the runner, the umpire should not make a loud call and use wild body English. If the outcome of the play is obvious to everyone in the ballpark, there's no reason to sell the call with a big show.

If, however, that play at first base is a bang-bang play, the umpire should ham it up a little bit. Be loud, and use big motions when you make that safe or out call. This not only shows everyone in the park what happened, but it also shows them that you are confident that you made the right call. By hamming it up, you're saying, "Look, folks, that might have been a close one, but I had a better view of the play than anyone, and *my call is right on!*"

Deep down, ballplayers and fans usually don't know for certain whether the man is safe or out. You have to sell them the idea that you *do* know.

If you oversell the obvious plays, people will think you're a showboat—or that you didn't have good enough judgment to know that the play's outcome was obvious. On the other hand, if you undersell the close plays, people will think you aren't sure you got it right.

Keep proportionality in mind throughout the game.

Signals between umpires

Especially with a two-man system, umpires should always do whatever they can to communicate with each other. They should remind each other of possible plays that could develop, such as the infield fly rule or a tag-up situation. They should be able to question each other about calls. And they should be able to indicate what parts of the diamond they will cover in certain situations.

Because the four-man system makes positioning easy, many major-league umpires do not bother using body signals to their crew's other umpires. For some reason, they think the constant back-and-forth between umpires looks undignified. But I use umpire's signals for one simple reason: communicating with the other umpires keeps me in the game. If I know I have to remind my crew members about a possible bunt play, that keeps my attention on the game. I am able to anticipate plays better.

I think umpires at all levels should develop a set of signals for internal communication. Especially in amateur leagues—where

inexperienced players and unfamiliar umpires and teams abound
—the signals are vital in helping the umpire stay involved in the
game.

When you use signals, keep them as discreet as possible. Unlike the signals you use to call a runner out at the plate, the internal signals are meant to be understood by the umpires, not
everyone in the park. The players should not have the benefit of
knowing what you're thinking about on your job. They are on the
field to play baseball *as removed from the umpires as posible.* The
spotlight should always be on the players.

Here are a few situations where signals between umpires
might be useful, along with some suggested signals, when one
umpire wants to tell his partner:

- "I'm going to cover another base." With a man on first base,
  you might see the plate umpire move a raised finger in a cir-
  cle. He'll be telling the field umpire that he will go out to
  cover plays at third base on a hit—and the field umpire should
  be ready to cover the plate.
- "I'm staying here to watch a possible play." By pointing to the
  ground, either the plate or field umpire will indicate that he
  cannot stray too far from his area because a play could develop
  there quickly.
- "It's an infield fly situation." Point in the air.
- "I have a question about the batter's checked swing." When a
  catcher disputes the plate umpire's ball call on a checked
  swing, the plate umpire should point to the field umpire and
  ask for a second opinion. If the field umpire thought the batter
  took a swing at the ball, he should make an out signal. If he
  thinks the batter did not swing, he should make a safe signal.
- "I need your attention." By patting the top of his cap, an
  umpire attracts the other's attention. The first umpire might
  want to meet between innings, point out foreign objects on the
  field, or ask him to shift his position.

Both umpires should agree upon a set of signals before each
game. Other signals certainly can be added, and one or two on
my list might not be very useful in your league. The important

thing is to find a way to communicate discreetly throughout the game.

Besides using these body signals, the umpires should communicate verbally. When you cover a rundown play, shout out what part of the field you're covering. When there's a play in the outfield, shout out whether or not you're going out.

FIVE
The Plate Umpire

Visitors to the major-league umpire dressing rooms frequently comment on the differences in the way the four umpires prepare for games. As three of the umpires relax, amiably chatting and joking, the fourth man always seems to be a little uptight. If that fourth man is not cold and detached from his umpiring partners, he acts like a crazy man, shouting insults, interrupting his partners, and generally raising a ruckus.

If that fourth umpire is a little moody or a little hyperactive, his partners have no trouble forgiving him. They are understanding because they know the oddball is simply trying to deal with the pressures of the day's assignment—calling a game behind home plate. The home plate umpire's job is one of the toughest.

Among the major leagues' biggest plate umpire maniacs are Marty Springstead and Larry McCoy. The late Nestor Chylack also was an animal before his plate assignments. Durwood Merrill is probably the most pensive (read: moody) man before a plate appearance.

What makes the plate umpire's job so grueling is mostly the physical chore of calling almost 300 balls and strikes from a crouched position behind home plate over a period of two to three hours. Like the pitcher and the catcher, the plate umpire has to be on top of every pitch. The difference is that he is not allowed any rest or mistakes. He'll hear from the players and coaches whenever they think he misses a pitch.

As he calls the game's 300 pitches, the plate umpire takes a beating. If the catcher misses a pitch, the ball pounds the umpire on his mask or chest, or, worse, an unprotected part of his body. If the batter fouls a pitch toward the dirt, the ball stings the umpire on his shin or foot. If the batter fouls the ball back, the catcher will throw his mask down to chase the ball, and the mask frequently lands right in the path that the umpire must travel to see the play.

At the same time the plate umpire bobs up and down behind the plate and takes the beating of foul tips and arguments from players, he must also be in command of the game's other aspects. As the game's "umpire in chief," the plate umpire is responsible for everything that happens in the game—setting ground rules and rubbing up baseballs before the game, setting the pace of the action and settling rule disputes during the game, deciding whether a game should be postponed or ended because of bad weather, and turning in game reports to the league president after the game.

The plate umpire's job is the most important job on the field. He deserves all the understanding he can get from his partners.

The pregame routine

The job actually begins well before the game. Because he is going to be in charge of the game, the plate umpire should arrive at the field about thirty minutes before game time.

He should inspect the field and determine how to deal with the strange situations that might develop because of field conditions. What happens when a ball gets stuck in an outfield fence? Should the bullpen be considered in or out of play? What if some spectators watch the game from the field and the ball is hit toward the spectators in fair territory?

The best approach, I think, is to look around the field from one side to the other with the coaches. Ask the coaches if they have any questions about or problems with the various parts of the park.

In addition to anticipating the tough plays that might develop in a game, the plate umpire should also inspect the ballpark for other problem areas.

About five minutes before game time, the umpires meet with

the coaches of the two teams at home plate to discuss ground rules
and exchange lineup cards. Once the plate umpire gives the managers copies of their opponents' lineup cards, he has complete control
of the game. He has authority over everyone on the field and in
the stadium, including the home team, the hot dog vendor, and
other employees of the stadium. Everyone. The umpire-in-chief is
responsible for delaying, postponing, and cancelling games. He is
the representative of the league. If anyone in the stadium defies
the umpire-in-chief, he faces discipline from the school, association,
or league office.

If you have already worked with the coaches and the field,
the plate conference shouldn't last long. Because the home team
plays half of its games on that field, its coach should be allowed
to take the lead in suggesting the ground rules. If the coaches disagree about how to deal with idiosyncratic plays, the plate umpire
should step in to make the final decision.

ON ROAD—OFFICIAL BATTING ORDER

CLUB **LOS ANGELES**   DATE_____

	ORIGINAL		CHANGE	ALSO ELIGIBLE
1	Rivers 8	B	Blair	
		C		
2	white 7	B	Thomson	
		C		
3	Munson 2	B		
		C		
4	Jackson DH	B		
		C		
5	Piniella 9	B	Johnstone	
		C		
6	Nettles 5	B		
		C		
7	Spencer 3	B		
		C		
8	Doyle 4	B		
		C		
9	Dent 6	B		
		C		
	Hunter 1	D	Gosse	
		E		

MANAGER'S SIGNATURE___B. Lemon___

OFFICIAL BATTING ORDER

CLUB **LOS ANGELES**   DATE _10-17-78_

	ORIGINAL		CHANGE	ALSO ELIGIBLE
1	Lopes	B		
		C		
2	Russell	B		
		C		
3	Smith	B		
		C		
4	Garvey	B		
		C		
5	Cey	B		
		C		
6	Baker	B		
		C		
7	Monday	B		
		C		
8	Ferguson	B		
		C		
9	Davalillo (DH)	B		
		D	Welch	
	Sutton (P)	E	Rau	

MANAGER'S SIGNATURE___Tom Lasorda___

*The first thing you will notice is that the Yankees forgot to
bring their lineup cards for the Series. What is important to the
umpire is that he has the starting lineup and all substitutions
throughout the game.*

Some leagues have strict rules about substitutions: no player who has been removed from a game may reenter the game, and no player who is not on the roster may play in a game. For this reason, the plate umpire should ask coaches not only for the starting lineups, but also for a list of players who start the game on the bench. That list will help the umpire stay on top of the game.

Setting the pace of the game

Because the home plate umpire is involved in every pitch, and because both teams recognize him as the umpires' crew chief, the plate umpire must set a positive tone for the game. The game must move quickly. As I've said before, everybody on the field is more alert when the game is brisk. And the plate umpire can make a big difference in setting the game's pace.

The crew chief should make sure the game starts on time. There is nothing wrong with the plate umpire admonishing the teams to hurry up a little to get things going. A chipper "Okay, fellows, let's get the game going" will help set a positive, aggressive tone for the game. A nice crisp call on the first pitch of the game will also help.

Give the count every two or three pitches during the game. Most players probably know what the situation is, but constant reminders keep everyone sharp. They keep the game moving at a brisk pace.

Both the pitcher and batter will delay the game from time to time. The batter should be permitted to occasionally step out of the batter's box to get ready for the pitch, but he should not be permitted to interrupt the flow of the game with his antics. If you feel he is abusing his privilege, refuse to grant him time out. If he refuses to get in the batter's box, order the pitcher to throw the ball and call a strike every time he does. The rules allow such a tactic, and it'll get the game going pronto. I have had to use this rule only a couple of times—with Amos Otis of the Pittsburgh Pirates and Lloyd Moseby of the Toronto Blue Jays. The plate stallers are usually well known in any league. Be ready for them.

The pitcher also delays the game with his meditation on the hill. With the bases empty, the rules require the pitcher to throw the ball twenty seconds after receiving the ball. Second-base umpires in the major leagues carry stopwatches in their pockets to keep the pitcher on his toes. If the pitcher repeatedly takes longer than twenty seconds to throw a pitch when there are no base runners, call a ball. I think I've invoked this rule on two pitchers in my eleven years as a major-league umpire—with Steve Busby, a plodder, and Al Hrabosky, a psych-out artist.

Don't allow the pitchers to go to the other extreme—quick pitching. The batter should be allowed to get ready for each pitch. Some pitchers try to throw the ball almost right after they get the ball from the catcher to get the batter off stride. Jim Kaat made a comeback with the Phillies at age forty when he caught batters off stride with his quick pace. Don't let the pitcher put the batter at an unfair disadvantage.

Remind the players of the count every two or three pitches. Giving the count not only keeps the players alert, it also keeps you alert behind the plate. Even though all big-league parks display the count on a scoreboard, American League umpires like Rich Garcia and Jimmy Evans frequently give the count as a way of staying involved in the game.

Balloon or not balloon

For years, two distinct groups of home plate umpires worked baseball games—balloon umpires and inside umpires. One group tended to call a "high" strike zone, and the other called a "low" strike zone. One moved somewhat clumsily, and the other was able to get into position with ease.

"Balloon umpire" and "inside umpire," refer to the kind of chest protector that the plate umpire uses to shield himself. The balloon protector is simply a huge slab of foam rubber that the umpire holds in front of himself during pitches—a place for the umpire to hide to avoid the punishing blows of missed pitches and foul tips. The inside protector, worn underneath the plate umpire's uniform, is little more than a catcher's chest protector with shoulder pads.

The inside protectors are easier to transport to games, which makes them attractive to umpires of amateur league games. They fit inside a small bag; the balloons of old practically require a van to transport.

But more important than getting the protector to the game is what the protector allows the umpire to do during the game. The inside protector is easier to use. The umpire with a balloon protector positions himself with his head right above the catcher's head. An umpire with an inside protector can get down lower, closer to the catcher (and the action), and move slightly to a side. Moving down low and to the side is important, because it means that he can better see low pitches, as well as pitches on the inside part of the plate.

I'm convinced that the inside protector allows the umpire to call a more consistent game. The balloon is just too bulky to allow the umpire to get and stay in the same position for every pitch. You never have to think about the inside protector once you put it on—and you can concentrate better on calling balls and strikes.

The inside protector also allows the umpire to move around the field better. Baseball's two professional umpire schools used to teach their students a complicated set of maneuvers for removing the mask and balloon protector, holding them with one hand, and running to see a play develop in the field. The maneuvers weren't easy, and the schools' practice sessions for handling the balloons were comical. Watching those students run with that mattress was like watching Dick Van Dyke stumble on the stairs in the old TV sitcom. Umpires are lucky that the inside protector eliminates such clumsiness.

Almost all umpires today use the inside protectors. American

League umpires used the balloon protector until 1976, when league officials decided to switch to the inside protector. A few big-league umpires still use the balloon, but everyone else has made smooth transitions to the inside protector.

Use of the balloon protector accounted for the American League's reputation as a "high strike" league. Most major-league players will tell you that the two leagues' umpires now call basically the same strike zone since the move to inside protectors. Anything that makes umpires' calls more consistent is good.

Use of the inside protector has one great advantage for amateur leagues: it helps umpires move beyond their natural fears of taking a beating behind the plate. With the balloon, there was always a place to hide. With the inside protector, every plate umpire realizes he must stay on top of the game and completely conquer his fears of getting hurt. Inside protectors help devleop courage.

Getting set for the pitch

Preparing to watch pitches is the most fundamental part of the home plate umpire's job. How you do it depends on the kind of protector you use.

The umpire who uses the inside protector straddles behind the catcher, just to the catcher's side where the batter is standing. When you crouch behind the catcher, plant your feet as far apart as your shoulders. When you bend down, bend your knees, not your waist. When a right-handed hitter is batting, put your left foot forward and point it toward the pitcher; when a left-handed hitter is batting, put your right foot forward. If you point your feet toward the pitcher, you won't be hurt by balls batted sharply back toward the dirt.

Some beginning umpires almost take their jobs too seriously. They get tight and hold their backs straight and perpendicular to the ground. Toward the end of the game, they find themselves exhausted by their rigid stance. What's worse is that their calls become inconsistent. Try to keep your back relaxed, with about 80 percent of the weight of the body leaning forward toward the pitch. Hold your hands loosely on the inside of the legs; if the hands are rigid and a ball hits them, there is greater chance that bones will break.

Getting set for the pitch when the batter is right-handed ...

... and when the batter is left-handed.

The umpire should crouch down low, with his head only slightly higher than the catcher's head. Most umpires say they see the strike zone best when they hold their heads at the top part of the strike zone because it's easier to see pitches that are slightly below, rather than above, their zones of vision. Keep your eyes level to the ground. You should follow the pitch with your eyes, not your head, and you can't do this well if your eyes are off to one side.

When you call balls and strikes, get as close as possible to the catcher. Depending on the level of play, umpires sometimes get so close to catchers that they actually rest their hands on the catcher's back. However, I do not believe this is a good practice, and I do not teach it at my umpire school.

A growing number of umpires have taken to using one knee stance. By resting their weight almost completely on the knee—the right knee for a right-handed batter, the left knee for a left-handed batter—the plate ump eliminates the strain and tension of the rigid crouch. As I indicated before, some baseball people think the knee stance is lazy, but I have used it and found that it keeps me calm and helps my concentration Yes, it's relaxing. When you're relaxed, you're more likely to call a good game. And you'll still have plenty of time to get up and around the field.

The umpire who uses the balloon protector stands directly behind the catcher, with his head directly above the catcher's head. He should spread his feet a little wider than his shoulders and hold the protector directly under the mask.

If you feel uncomfortable or if you feel bad about the calls you've been making, shift your position a little behind the plate. Batters often find that a slight change in their stance helps them to see the ball better. You sometimes will, too. It's nothing more than a way of getting a fresh start mentally as well as physically.

Never change your stance from pitch to pitch, though. I have seen young umpires assume different positions behind the plate depending on the game situations. Some will get down on their knees with no base runners, then get in the crouch when there are men on base. They figure that they can get away with the more comfortable knee position only when they do not have to move around the field. Invariably, these guys end up calling slightly different strikes in the different positions. With the exception of a one-time shift to see pitches better, do not use different stances behind the plate.

Seeing the pitches

The strike zone includes any pitch that goes over the plate between the batter's armpits to his knees *when the batter takes his natural stance*. The last phrase is important because many batters try to work out walks by assuming an unnaturally small stance and restricting their strike zone. Rickey Henderson of the New York Yankees and Pete Rose of the Cincinnati Reds are both notorious for these antics. How do you tell if a batter's stance is natural? Watch the batter as he swings the bat on a pitch. Those players who crouch down low for a smaller strike zone will usually stand up a little to take their cuts. That's the batter's natural stance.

The plate umpire should imagine the strike zone as a pentagonal (five-sided) box covering that area. Any pitch that cuts any part of the box—even if only part of the ball cuts the box—is a strike. What matters is not where the ball ends up—where the catcher's glove is after the pitch—but where the pitch crossed home plate in relation to the strike zone.

Different leagues have slightly different strike zones, according to the level of play. In many youth leagues, the pitchers have a difficult time controlling their pitches, so the strike zone might be a little larger than it would be in a professional league. If the umpire is working a game in a new league where the zone might be different, he should talk to the coaches or other league umpires before the game about the strike zone.

Pitches that hit near the low part of the strike zone and the inside part of the zone are the plate umpire's toughest calls. When a batter recoils from the plate on an inside strike, it's hard to tell him that the ball hit the inside corner. And when the ball hits the lowest part of the strike zone, it's hard to tell the batter that he should have swung because the pitch is so difficult to hit. But both pitches are strikes. Don't let your sympathy for the batter allow you to call those strikes balls.

The plate umpire should try to see the ball move all the way from the pitcher's hand through the strike zone. The Jack Nicklaus method—imagining the ball's movement as it heads toward its destination—can be as useful for a plate umpire as for a professional golfer. Imagine the ball coming in the strike zone, on a track as wide as the plate and as high as the distance from the batter's armpits to his knees. If the ball stays on the track all the way to the plate, it's a strike. If it becomes derailed, it's a ball.

I cannot stress enough the need for the plate umpire to hold his head still during the pitch. The umpire should follow the ball through or outside the imaginary box *with his eyes only*. If he moves his body in with the pitch, he most likely will take his eyes off the ball long enough to miss the pitch. Remember what we said earlier about dynamic visual acuity: it allows you to take full measure of moving objects without jerking your head around. Calling pitches is a matter of split seconds, so you need all the time you can get.

If you stay still when you make ball-strike calls, you have to have extremely bad judgment to blow a lot of calls. But if you're moving when you make those calls, you have to have great judgment to get most of the calls right.

Besides putting you at a disadvantage in making the ball-strike calls, moving around the plate also chips away at your confidence. You never really know for sure whether you make the right calls. That lack of confidence is bound to affect your whole game.

Consistency is the most important aspect of umpiring behind the plate. To be consistent requires intense concentration and confidence. During the umpire strike of 1979, the major leagues hired some minor-league and college umpires to call the big-league games. Players and managers complained that the umpires started to call different pitches during the last three innings of the games. The temporary umpires usually did quite well for six innings—but after that they got nervous and made inconsistent calls because of the greater importance they thought their decisions had. The lesson is to concentrate and be the same umpire throughout the game.

Try to establish a rhythm when you are behind the plate. There will be games when pitchers throw inconsistently, runners get caught in rundowns, and fielders boot the most routine plays, and that will adversely affect your rhythm. Like the elite athlete, you must work to stay in the game even when the flow of the game changes dramatically and you're not all there physically and emotionally.

In almost any amateur league, you have to be ready for all kinds of pitches. Younger pitchers tend to have poor control, which, combined with their catcher's relative lack of experience, means that the plate umpire finds himself getting pounded with errant pitches. Older pitchers throw the full range of pitches found in the major leagues, from the good old-fashioned fastball right down to the knuckle-curveball and screwball. Umpires in advanced leagues should be ready for breaking pitches.

A good umpire talks to himself during the game. He gives himself little reminders so that his attention does not wander, which certainly can happen over the course of 300 pitches. He asks himself if his head is moving. He reminds himself to crouch low. He tells himself to be ready for plays that might develop if the ball is hit, such as a play at the plate. If he thinks he might be rushing calls, he reminds himself to call the pitch once silently before shouting out the call and making the proper motion.

The plate umpire's other concerns

The home plate umpire, of course, must deal with several hundred calls on balls and strikes. Here are some other tough concerns for the plate umpire:

* *Helping the field umpire.* On top of all the problems he has at the backstop, the plate umpire frequently has to cover for his partner in the field.

   The plate umpire should be ready to move around the diamond after every batted ball. When the batter hits the ball and there are no base runners, the plate umpire should move to the front part of the diamond between the mound and the plate. When base runners are aboard, the plate umpire should move just to the foul side of the third-base line, ready to cover plays at third base and home plate.

   The plate umpire also should be ready to make calls when the field umpire's vision is blocked on tag plays, when a fielder makes a swipe tag on the batter going to first base, and on possible infield fly rule situations.

- *Hit batsman or foul ball.* Deciding whether a batter has been hit—and is therefore entitled to a free pass to first base—is an easy task about nine times out of ten. You see the pitch veering into the batter, and you hear the ball smack against the player's arm or leg.

     But some pitches are tough to see—most notably the high inside fastball. If a pitch just brushes the hitter, you might never know. In the old days, when players wore those billowing cotton uniforms, it was more difficult. But that's little solace to today's umpire. What to do?

     In most close cases, take your tip from the player in the split second right after the pitch. Most players don't think fast enough to fake being hit with a pitch. If the batter immediately clutches a damaged limb, chances are he was hit. If the batter lingers around the plate, chances are he wasn't hit.

     What if you call a ball and the player argues that he was hit? Is there anything the player can do to prove he has been hit? Not much. The player can show the umpire the red mark that the ball's impact left on his hand or arm. If there is a red mark on the part of the body that was closest to the pitch, the umpire should change his ruling.

     Perhaps the most famous dispute over a hit batsman took place in the 1969 World Series between the New York Mets and the Baltimore Orioles. Cleon Jones of the Mets claimed he was hit on the shoe by a pitch, and his manager, Gil Hodges, showed the umpires a ball with a black smudge of shoe polish. Jones got his pass to first base, and Hodges later joked that he kept a supply of smudged balls in the dugout for such occasions.

     I was involved in a play in 1981 that illustrates the difficulty of the call. Damaso Garcia of the Toronto Blue Jays was batting, and he received an inside pitch. As he recoiled from the plate, the ball moved in on him, and then went bouncing away. I ruled that he fouled the pitch off. He argued that he had been hit and deserved a free pass to first base, but I stood my ground.

     The next day, I saw Garcia before the game. His hand was in a cast, broken from the pitch that I said he fouled off. I had made a mistake.

     All an umpire can do is to make sure he sees the ball come all the way from the pitcher's hand to the plate. As I have said before, the umpire has an advantage over the batter and catcher because he can watch the pitch all the way from the mound to the plate.

The umpire should also listen intently as he watches. What's the sound as the ball bounds away from the batter—the sound of a bat or bone? The distinction is easy to discern when the batter uses an aluminum bat, but not so easy when the batter uses a wooden bat.

Sometimes the field umpire has a better view of the play. Make eye contact with your partner. See if he saw the play well enough to make a call—he was, after all, looking at the batter from the front—a better angle. If he nods and you are uncertain about your call, point to him and ask him to make a call.

- *The bouncing ball.* When the batter hits the ball and it bounces into the air near home plate, it's tough to see whether the ball is fair or foul. Most players do not realize that home plate is in fair territory, and that any ball that hits the plate is in play. The question is whether or not such a "topped ball" stays in play.

To judge if a topped ball stays fair, move a few steps to the foul side of the first- or third-base lines near the plate. By looking down the foul lines, you'll be able to see where the ball is when a player picks it up.

When the batter hits the ball down on his feet and the ball lands in fair territory, the ball is still foul. The plate umpire should make that call quickly and explain that when a batted ball hits the batter it's foul, so there's no confusion.

- *The squeeze play.* Luckily for the umpire, the squeeze play is almost a relic. Before the days of the long ball, the squeeze play was an integral part of a baseball team's strategy for deliberately "manufacturing" runs. Ty Cobb typified the era when a common way to score a run was to get a single, order that runner to steal second base, sacrifice the runner to third base, and score the runner with a squeeze or suicide squeeze play.

Teams from high-school leagues to the major leagues pay little attention to that offensive strategy these days. They would rather believe the "big bang" theory of Baltimore Orioles Manager Earl Weaver, who said most games are won with big hits like three-run homers and two-run doubles.

The umpire should know what to do on a squeeze play, though. Squeeze plays occur three or four times a year—usually right in the middle of a pennant race, when games count the most.

The first thing to remember is to make the strike or ball call if the batter misses the pitch. Whether or not the pitch hits the strike zone could determine whether the squeeze attempt even matters. Many teams will attempt the squeeze play before full counts because the risks then are minimal.

After you've made the ball-strike call, look toward the runner. Step to the side if possible. As with all tag plays, shift to an angle where you can frame the main components of the play—the catcher, runner, and base. Watch the *ball* and *the part of the body* that the catcher is attempting to tag. Make sure the catcher holds on to the ball. Watch for possible interference by the batter, runner, or catcher. Make the call quickly.

- *Steal of home plate.* Stealing home is another of baseball's lost arts, but it might be experiencing a revival. Teams at all levels run more these days than they have in decades. Coaches are not excessively concerned anymore about risking a base runner if there is a worthwhile reward for the risk.

Stealing home requires intense concentration on the part of the base runner. The base runner's goal is to beat the pitch to home plate. He'll usually dance off third base for a few pitches, perhaps drawing some pickoff throws from the pitcher and catcher. He makes his mad dash for the plate just as the pitcher starts his slow windup, the catcher lazily lobs the ball back to the pitcher after a pitch, or the pitcher throws to third base in a pickoff attempt.

In most cases, other plays will also be happening at the same time. If the play to steal home occurs during a pitch, the plate umpire must make a ball-strike call as well as the safe-out call at home plate. The plate umpire must also watch for possible obstruction, offensive and defensive interference, the runner going out of the baselines, and the runner getting hit by the ball.

The plate umpire should try to step back a little as the play on the base runner is made. He needs to get the most complete picture of the play, which means moving slightly to one side if possible, to frame the picture. The umpire should watch the catcher for his reaction to the play, and position himself accordingly. Once the play is made, the umpire makes the calls in the order they happened—the ball-strike call first, then the safe-out call.

Attempted steals of home often are part of a larger play—
a double steal or a bluffed double steal. The plate umpire and
his partner in the field should make sure they cover all plays.

- *Infractions by the pitcher and catcher.* The plate umpire is most
responsible for watching for a possible balk call. If the pitcher
steps toward the plate and throws to first base, or vice versa,
call a balk.

  The plate umpire should also watch for other infractions
such as doctored pitches, quick pitches, lengthy delays, or failure to maintain contact with the pitching rubber.

  Also watch the catcher for possible interference with the
batter's swing. Especially with men on base or on a crucial
pitch, catchers tend to lean forward. If they touch the batter,
it's catcher's interference, and the batter should get a free pass
to first base.

- *The batter.* The plate umpire is responsible for making sure
the batter stays in the batter's box throughout his swing. If a
foot moves outside the box, the batter is out. If you're watching
the pitch like you're supposed to, it's hard to keep your eye on
the batter's feet. Just make sure the batter's feet are in the
box at the beginning of each pitch.

  A lot of hitters like to stand way back in the batter's box
to get a little extra time to see the pitches. Cal Ripken, Jr., is
a prime example. He gets in there and starts kicking dirt over
the chalk lines. Make sure you know where the lines should be
even if they're rubbed out, and make the player stay in the
box.

  While you're at it, check the hitter's bat. Does it have too
much pine tar on it? Does it show any other signs of being doctored to increase its punch—such as clear cuts in the bat that
might indicate that the bat was cut for cork insertion? If there
are indications, the bat should be removed from the game. Also
check to see that the batter is wearing a helmet.

  Watch for possible interference by the batter. Sometimes
the bat will get in the catcher's way as the catcher attempts to
grab or throw the ball.

Evaluating the plate umpires

All of the students at the Joe Brinkman Umpire School work
under the critical eyes of about a dozen instructors. No matter
where the students are, the instructors will be close behind them

with a clipboard, taking notes. We use these notes to grade the umpires and decide whether to recommend them for jobs in professional baseball.

Evaluating the plate umpires

```
JOE BRINKMAN                    PLATE  EVALUATION              FL - CA
UMPIRE SCHOOL
          Student:  LCNO            Instructor: STAFF
          Date:        7/2/84       Game:  FINAL

                              GOOD      AVERAGE      POOR
  . Field Presence             ✓         ___         __
  _____
  . Voice                      ✓         ___         __
  _____
  . Stance                    ___         ✓          __
  _____
  . Movement from behind plate ___        ✓          __
   CAN'T GO IN TO RUNDOWN WHEN RUNDOWN GOING TO 1ST
  . Position on Fair/Foul Balls ___       ✓          __
   STAYS W/ PLAY AT 1ST
  . Position on Plays           ✓        ___         __
  _____
  . Judgement of Pitches       ___        ✓          __
  _____
  . Movement on Pitches        ___        ✓          __
  _____
  . Communication w/partner     ✓        ___         __
  _____
  . Timing                     ___        ✓          __
  _____
  . Hustle                      ✓        ___         __
  _____
  . Game Control                ✓        ___         __

    RUNDOWN - MISSED OBSTRUCTION      LATE REACTION TO THROWS
  General Comments:                   NO TIME PLAY REACTION
      BAT HITTING BALL - GOOD
    WENT TO 3RD ON THROW TO 2ND - GUESSING
    STANDING AT BALL  NOT GLANCING AT RUNNERS
```

Here's an evaluation of a student's field mechanics working behind the plate.

SIX
The Field Umpire

From the lowest levels of Little League Baseball to the Class AA professional leagues, almost every organized baseball league uses a variation of the two-man umpiring system. Many leagues use the three-man system during important contests—a league championship series, for example, or an all-star game. Almost all organized baseball and softball games are called by two-man crews. When one part of a two-man umpiring crew cannot make it to the game and the league officials cannot find a replacement, one umpire has complete responsibility for calling games.

Many leagues don't use a formal system, as such. They leave the system for calling games up to the individual crews. Often, newcomers to umpiring are brought into a league's umpiring corps with the help of an experienced umpire. The rookie umpire adopts the style of his or her mentor, and in subsequent years will train other newcomers in that style.

In umpiring, as in almost every other avocation, there isn't always a right way and a wrong way. An umpiring crew's style should depend on the physical and intellectual abilities of the two umpires who make up that crew. If one umpire is particularly agile, for example, it might make sense to have that umpire run a little more. Maybe that umpire should cover a greater share of the baseball diamond, while his partner lends his own abilities.

Whatever the different abilities of the two umpires, however, crews should try to split the responsibilities as evenly as possible.

The umpires are, after all, a team. They should have the same amount of hustle and support.

Because I am usually teaching more than one hundred of them at a time and I need a fair way to evaluate their abilities, I insist that all of the students at the Joe Brinkman Umpire School learn and use one system for two-man-crew umpiring. But using the system allows me to do more than grade the students.

It also instills confidence in every umpire who uses it. Many times, you'll be umpiring with a complete stranger. If all the umpires in a league work under the same system, they will know who's covering what part of the diamond every time a play develops. There's no guesswork. An ad hoc umpiring system works well enough about 95 percent of the time; it's usually pretty obvious who can get in position to cover a given play. But that other 5 percent of the plays is going to give you headaches if you don't have a system.

If you can, try to use the system we have developed at the umpire school. It might make sense to alter some of the specifics according to different levels of skill and the rules of the league.

The two-man system

Under the two-man system, one umpire works behind the plate while the partner works from three basic positions in the infield, depending on the number of base runners.

The field umpire appears to have a pretty easy job; indeed, if that field umpire can get into good position on all the plays he can get through a game with little wear and tear. But getting in a good position to see plays is not always very easy, especially with the two-man system. It requires a lot of running and thinking ahead. In most amateur leagues, the players make a lot of errors, which means the umpire has to make several calls in both the outfield and infield. Umpiring on the bases can be exhausting.

The field umpire has three basic positions. When there are no base runners, the field umpire stands about ten to fifteen feet behind the first baseman, just on the foul side of the right-field line. If the first baseman is playing at the edge of the outfield grass, the field umpire needs to stand only ten feet behind him.

When there is a runner on first base, the umpire stands just

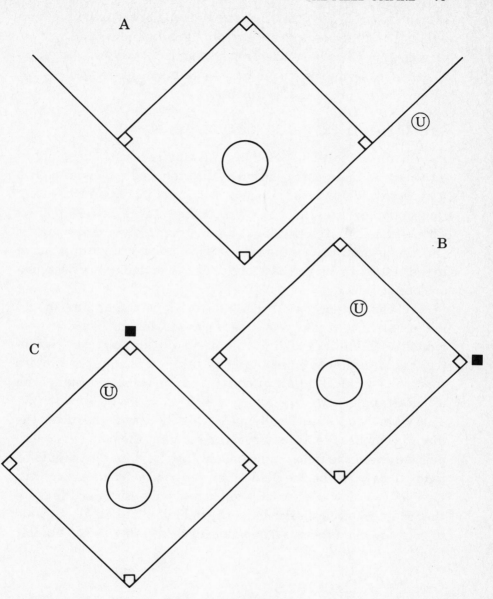

With no base runners, the field umpire (A) stands on the right-field line, about ten or fifteen feet beyond the first baseman. If there's a man on first base, the field umpire (B) will stand in front of second base, not quite halfway between the baseline and the pitcher's mound. If there's a runner on second, the umpire (C) will move over to the other side of second base.

in front of and to the first-base side of second base—not quite half-way between the baseline and the pitcher's mound. With a runner on second or third base, the umpire stands just in front of and to the third-base side of second base—again, not quite halfway between the baseline and the mound.

Getting ready for the play

In all three infield positions, the umpire faces home plate in either the standing set position or the crouched set position. The umpire should watch the pitcher's motion before turning his attention to home plate. He should watch the pitcher for a sign of an illegal action. With or without base runners, the umpire makes sure the pitcher touches the rubber and doesn't do anything illegal to the ball. With men on base, the umpire will make sure the pitcher doesn't balk.

As the pitcher goes through his motions, the umpire should make a practice of taking one step forward when there are no base runners. He should watch the pitcher make his delivery, then direct his attention to home plate. By taking the step, the umpire tends to stay alert on all pitches and can see batted balls from a better angle.

When the pitcher finally makes his delivery to the hitter, the umpire watches the hitter. From time to time, the home plate umpire will need the field umpire's help. The field umpire should be ready to help. When the field umpire is behind first base, he will have a good view of checked swings and balls hit near the plate that could go either fair or foul. The field umpire will also be able to help out when there is a question about whether or not a batter is hit with a pitch.

Game situations

Here are general instructions for the field umpire for several game situations:

If there are no base runners, the field umpire stands behind first base . . . If a ball is hit on the ground to an infielder, get in position to watch the throw or the unassisted putout. The best angle to watch all throws is on a line perpendicular to the line of the throw. Unfortunately, you can't always get the ninety-degree view, but get as close to ninety degrees as possible.

On a typical ground ball to an infielder, the field umpire should move behind the line of the throw from the infielder to the first baseman. When the shortstop makes a throw from the hole, the field umpire will be about seven or eight feet down the line from first base to second base. When the third baseman makes a throw from the bag, the umpire will stand further inside the infield.

There will be a few times when you shouldn't use the ninety-degree angle position. For example, if a ball is hit to the second baseman's left, you would have to be in foul territory to get the ninety-degree angle view, unless you were able to move all the way into the infield. You'd also be standing behind the first baseman and wouldn't have a good view of the ball and base runner arriving at the bag.

If you took that ninety-degree stance in foul territory, you would be in a bad position to get to other plays that might develop. If a fielder misplays the ball and the runner attempts to reach

The field umpire's position when there are no base runners.

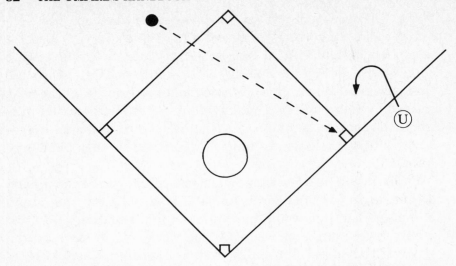

Try to see plays at first base from a ninety-degree angle twelve to eighteen feet from the base. This angle and distance will help you to see the whole play clearly.

second base, you have a long way to run to see a play at second base. Chances are you'd be out of position for the play at second base. So when the second baseman moves to his left for the ground ball, watch the play closer to first base than normal. You'll still have a pretty good view of the play, and you'll be able to hustle to second base, too.

Situations like this point to one basic lesson: always think ahead to the next possible play. Don't put yourself in a good position for one play at the risk of being out of position for a subsequent play.

Never get too close to the throw. You will not get as good a view of a play involving a throw if you are right on top of that play. Try to get into a position where you can see all of the factors involved in the play—the bag, the runner as he approaches the bag, and the fielders as they approach the bag.

Also, if you are too close to the play, that play could "explode" on you. If there is a collision at first base, if the fielder drops the ball, or if one of the players falls down, you could find yourself an unwitting participant in the play. It's best to stay as far away as possible.

When the batter hits a ground ball, watch the ball until the fielder fields the ball and releases the throw. By the time the first baseman or another player covering first base reaches out for the catch, you should already be in the set position and ready to watch the play carefully.

Forgive me if I sound like a broken record, but be absolutely still when you watch the play. If you move just your head, there is a real danger that you will lose track of the play for the split second that the play takes to be completed. Just as it is difficult to hit a moving target, it is difficult to hit a stationary target if you are moving.

The only way to make a call at first base is to watch the bag and listen for the sound of the ball hitting the glove of the fielder at first base. If you hear the ball hit the glove before the runner's foot hits the bag, the runner is out. Otherwise, the runner is safe. Also watch the bag for the fielder's foot. To record the out, he must be touching the bag at the time he receives the throw.

In all plays, stay away from the traffic. You must be careful not to get in any player's way. For example, if the second baseman fields a ground ball, you could be in the line of the throw to the first baseman if you are not careful. Or if there is a foul ball between the plate and first base, you could conceivably bump into

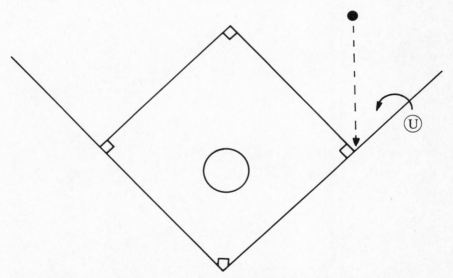

You won't always be able to get that ideal ninety-degree angle. If you got that angle on a throw from a deep second-base position, you'd be in the coach's box—and you wouldn't have much time to get to other parts of the field.

five players—the catcher, pitcher, first baseman, second baseman, and base runner.

When a play develops in the outfield . . . Occasionally, the batter will hit a ball that is just barely within the reach of the outfielders, and there is a question as to whether or not the fielder actually catches the ball. Outfielders often pretend that they catch a ball on the fly when they actually trap the ball or catch it on a hop.

When the field umpire sees a catch-no-catch situation developing on a fly ball to the right side of the outfield, he should run to the outfield to cover the play. He should yell out to the plate umpire that he's going, so the plate umpire will know that he is to cover first base.

If there are base runners, the umpire stands to the right of second base . . . With base runners, the field umpire's job becomes difficult. As always, he must be prepared to watch the routine play at first base, help the plate umpire on calls involving checked swings and foul balls that hit the batter, and go to the outfield for iffy catches. He must also watch the pitcher for signs of a balk, watch the first baseman and runner on pickoff attempts, watch

The field umpire's position with a runner at first base.

attempted steals of second base, be prepared to cover both bases on attempted sacrifice bunts, and make an occasional infield fly ruling.

On ground balls hit anywhere in the infield, the field umpire should take a step or two toward the mound to get a good angle on plays.

The umpire should follow the same principles on grounders that he follows with no base runners: try to get a ninety-degree angle view on the play, be ready to move on to another play, and stay out of the players' way.

Getting the ninety-degree angle view can be tough when you have to make more than one call, for example, on an attempted double play. Do the best you can. When you get set for the lead play at second base, think ahead to getting in good position for the subsequent play at first base.

With many ground balls where a base runner is on first base, the defense will try to turn a double play. When the fielders go to second base for a force play, make sure you see the whole play take place before making the call and getting set for the next play.

The field umpire's position with a runner at second base.

Don't turn your attention to first base before you decide and call the play at second base.

Try to be in the set position before making the call at both second base and first base. The only way you'll see a play well is to be absolutely still. If you find yourself making calls on the run, force yourself to stop and put your hands on your knees to watch the plays. If you feel it's necessary, grab your pant legs to stay in that set position. There will be enough time to see both plays.

There's a tendency to want to make a very quick call at second while turning toward the play at first base. Avoid that tendency. If you feel you're making your calls too fast—when the plays are still almost in progress—make the call to yourself, silently, before barking out the call to the players and spectators. Never rush a call.

Whenever there is a man on second base, men on first and second base or on first and third, or the bases are loaded, the field umpire should stand slightly to the right of second base on the inside of the diamond. He should also be more alert than ever.

In those situations, the field umpire often is responsible for

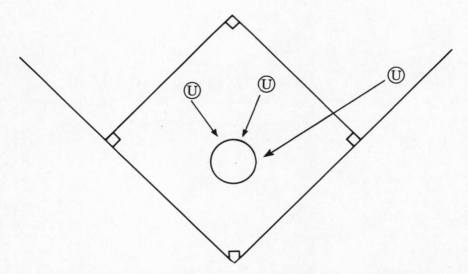

When what's happening on the field is confusing—as it often will be in amateur leagues—move just behind the mound so you can move in any direction. It's important to be able to get anywhere fast.

plays at all of the bases. That umpire often will be far away from the play he is calling. For example, with base runners at first and third, the pitcher might want to attempt a pickoff at first—and the umpire is almost all the way across the diamond. The field umpire can only anticipate which plays will develop and hope to get a good angle on them.

If the batter raps a clean hit but you are uncertain about what base is likely to be the site of a play, move to a position directly behind the pitcher's mound. That will enable you to move to any base where a play might develop. Make sure you watch the action around you—for example, the batter who gets a hit must touch first base as he rounds the bag—and be set to move anywhere on the diamond. Try to stand still, with your weight evenly distributed, so you are not leaning the wrong way.

Plays that might go to any base include bunts, balls that bounce high in front of home plate (these balls usually hit the plate), and "swinging bunts" or hits that do not get past the mound and present difficulty for the defense.

Other plays for the field umpire

Help the plate umpire.   Because he has a different angle on many pitches and plays near the backstop, the field umpire often can assist the plate umpire on a number of plays.

Especially when he stands down the first-base line, the field umpire often has the best view of the batter's checked swings. If the plate umpire calls a ball on a pitch in which the batter cuts his swing short, the coach may ask for a second opinion. The plate umpire points to the field umpire and asks, "Did he go?" The field umpire should immediately indicate with an out or safe sign whether the ball was a strike or ball.

The field umpire also has a better view of many balls hit down toward the dirt. These hits sometimes hit the batter, the plate, or sometimes hit the ground in either fair or foul territory. When you're working the field, watch these plays, and try to communicate with the plate umpire. If you see the batted ball hit the batter, call it foul.

Swipe tags along the first- and third-base lines often give the base umpire fits. If you don't compromise your position in the field, watch the runner and fielder for the swipe tag. The base umpire can ask the plate umpire for help.

By covering his plays efficiently, the field umpire can make the plate ump's job easier. The field umpire should try to make sure the plate umpire does not have to move too far from the back-stop area. The field umpire should try to call rundown plays alone and take as many plays at third base as possible. He should also be careful not to leave the plate umpire with too many responsibilities when he covers outfield plays.

Because he has fewer responsibilities, the field umpire should also try to think ahead and give regular reminders (talk and make signals) of game situations to his partner. Remind him that the infield fly rule may have to be invoked. Alert him to possible steal plays and tag plays. Point out players' idiosyncrasies, such as a pitcher's leg movements on pickoff attempts or a batter's tendency to move out of the batter's box.

Pickoff play. Probably the most difficult play for the field umpire to call is the pickoff play. On the pickoff attempt at first base, the

The pickoff play is one of the toughest under a two-man system. It's almost a matter of making an educated guess on the play because you have to be all the way across the diamond from the play. When the play develops, try to move toward first base and get a decent angle.

umpire has almost no angle on the play. He is standing on the line between first base and second base right behind the base runner who is trying to get back to first base. Because the play is sudden, it's hard to increase your angle. The best you can do is to "steal" a couple steps toward the pitcher's mound whenever a pickoff attempt seems likely. Spin around toward first base to watch the play.

Steal attempts. Another tough play is the attempted steal of second base (or other bases). The only place you can see the play is directly in front of second base. But you can't get in that position too soon or you'll get beaned with the catcher's throw.

To get in position and avoid getting hit with the ball, you must literally follow the ball to second base. It's a pivoting action. When you see the catcher preparing to make the peg, turn to watch the throw. Follow the ball as it cuts up the diamond; when the ball arrives near your position, whirl around to face second base, with your hands on your knees.

Phantom tag. Thanks to television, the phantom tag has become anything but a phantom phenomenon. The play is now a part of baseball from high-school leagues all the way up to the professional leagues. These amateur-league players watch major-league baseball on television, and they imitate what they see.

For the record, what they see is illegal.

The phantom tag occurs during the execution of the common second-to-first double play. The fielder covering the front end of the double play at second base—usually the second baseman or shortstop—does not actually touch the bag before he relays the ball to first base. Instead, the fielder casually sweeps past the bag with the ball in his hand and avoids dealing with the base runner's disconcerting slide into the bag.

Technically, the phantom tag is wrong. The person making the force play at second base *should touch the base while holding the ball and then make the relay to first base.*

But in many leagues, coaches and players like the phantom tag. It saves infielders from getting spiked. It reduces mistakes. It increases the number of double plays, which means quicker and more satisfying games.

Find out what your league officials and coaches think about

*When you're covering an attempted steal of second base, make
sure you see the whole play happen. Watch the ball move all the
way from the catcher's hand to the infielder's glove. Then get as
close to the play as possible. Both the fielder and the runner can
obscure what's happening with fakes, so you must have your
nose right in on the play.*

this practice. Some will ban the play. Others will shrug and say: "Well, that's baseball. Funny game, ain't it?"

If you're going to let infielders use the phantom tag, make sure they could easily make the play at second base. They should be close to the bag, holding the ball for at least a couple seconds, for you to call the runner out.

Don't call the out at second just because a force play exists and the player is holding the ball. Make the fielder make most of the play, and miss second base just so he can avoid the sliding base runner and complete the double play.

SEVEN
The Umpire's Jurisdiction

Perhaps the most difficult aspect of umpiring baseball with a two-man system is avoiding a slapstick routine.

There is so much ground to cover with only two umpires that the umpires have to make sure they know where they're going at all times, or else they'll stumble and bump into each other all over the place. If you've ever watched "The Three Stooges," you'll have an idea how confusing situations can become without clear advance thinking.

The professional Japanese baseball leagues have an interesting way of making sure their umpires know where they should be set to make calls on the field. While American leagues rotate umpires around the field—one man will work the plate one day, and the field the next—Japanese umpires work the same position for months, sometimes years, at a time. The younger umpires work the field and the more experienced umpires take on the tougher plate assignments. Not only do the Japanese umpires learn the responsibilities of their positions perfectly, but they are brought into the system gradually.

Whatever system your league uses, it's important to make sure you know where you should be stationed to make a call, to avoid both umpires covering a single play and also to avoid *no* umpires covering the play. Assigning reponsibility for making calls is easy in the major leagues, where umpires are set up in a four-man system; the major-league umpire rarely has to move far from his original position near a base. But other leagues cannot afford to pay four umpires. As a result, the two umpires these leagues usually use must have better coordination in getting into position.

Many amateur leagues do not require the plate and field umpires to formally divide their responsibilities. The feeling is that the umpires will be able to work out the best system for coverage on their own. After all, many pairs of umpires work together for years as crews, and they know their strengths and weaknesses. There is no way anyone can anticipate every series of plays that will develop on the baseball diamond, so why try?

Both of the umpire schools sanctioned by the National Association of Professional Baseball, however, *do* try to establish a system for jurisdiction of play coverage. The reason is simple: there is no way to teach some 200 or 300 people how to umpire if each person speaks his own language. By requiring use of a formal system, the schools are better able to work with the students and judge their performances.

Our outline of the umpires' division of responsibilities might not be perfect for every league or for every umpiring crew. Every umpire brings to the game a different set of abilities, and every league likes to use its umpires in its own way.

Using a formal division of responsibilities has many advantages. If two busy umpires need anything during a game, it's a sense that the game is under control. If one umpire knows exactly what his partner will do on a given play, the two umpires will be able to cover more ground and earn more respect from the teams involved. Umpiring is a profession that demands control; a formal system is the best way to achieve it.

Even though it might not be used in all leagues, the following division of responsibilities for two-man umpiring crews should be a useful place to start thinking about how umpires should work together.

The situation checklist

Even with a good division of responsibilities, both umpires should think about calls they might need to make during a series of plays. Here's what a "situation checklist" should include:

*   What is the physical condition and background of my partner?

How will my partner's condition affect where I have to get positioned?

- Where is the ball? Where is it likely to be thrown?
- Are there any bases I might have to watch for a tag play?
- Where will the play occur?
- What plays might need backing up?
- What rules govern this set of plays?
- Is there a "line of action," or a part of the field where most of the plays are likely to occur?
- Who is the cutoff man? Who is the relay man?
- How will the alignment of players shift after the first set of plays?
- What fielders don't have a definite base to cover and are therefore available to back up other plays?

The division of responsibility

Here is the way we suggest umpires divide their responsibilities on the field:

Fair or foul calls

With no base runners, the plate umpire should cover all balls hit down the left-field line. He's also responsible for covering any balls hit down the first-base line up to the base. The field umpire is responsible for all balls hit down the right-field line beyond first base.

When there are runners aboard, the plate umpire should handle all of the fair-foul calls. The field umpire can help with balls batted down that hit the batter, but he should otherwise concentrate on covering the bases.

Catch or no-catch

No one on base . . . The plate umpire will cover the third baseman, the shortstop, the pitcher, and all outfield unless the base umpire goes out.

The base umpire will cover the second baseman, the first baseman, and the outfield if he goes out.

Runners on base . . . The plate umpire will cover the pitcher, the first baseman, and the third baseman going toward the lines, right and left fielders toward the lines.

The base umpire will cover all balls hit between the first baseman and the third baseman straight in and right fielder and left fielder straight in.

Plays involving ground rules

The plate umpire, of course, has primary responsibility for all ground rules. The base umpire should also have a good idea where to place the runners. The main thing is to study out the play and make sure you put the runners on the proper bases.

Hits to left field and center field with no base runners

When the batter hits a possible single, double, or triple to left or center field, the home plate umpire covers the outfield and moves back home. The base umpire covers the batter-runner all the way to third.

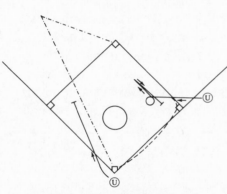

Single to left (nobody on base)

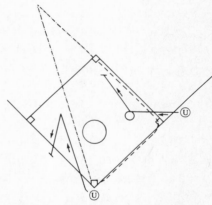

Double to left (nobody on base)

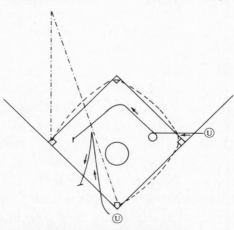

Triple to left (nobody on base)

Hits to right field with no base runners

When the batter hits the ball into right field and it seems it might go foul, or when the fielder has a chance to make a difficult play, the field umpire should follow the ball to the outfield. He should make the fair-foul call only when the ball hits the ground *beyond* first base; other fair-foul calls go to the plate umpire. After making your decision, move toward home plate to help your partner.

The plate umpire should move to the infield area around the mound, watching the runner touch first, staying ahead of him to second and possibly third.

When a runner moves from first to third base

<u>Base umpire</u>. When in the infield and the ball goes to the outfield, the base umpire turns with the ball and drops back to the mound. With a runner on first, he is responsible for the runner's touching second base and the batter-runner's touching first base. The base umpire is then responsible for the runner at second base—if he stops there—and the batter-runner on first. When the outfielder comes up throwing the ball, the baseman should react and go to the edge of the infield grass, about halfway between first and second base. From here if you see the ball go to second, you have a short distance to go to be on top of the play. If you see the ball go to first base, you've cut the distance you have to go to get to a play at first base. If the runner from first rounds second base and goes to third base, the play at third is the plate umpire's responsibility. You have only the batter-runner at first base. The most important thing you have to remember is watch the ball. It will force you to go where you have to be.

<u>Plate umpire</u>. The plate umpire is responsible for the runner from first base *if both he and the ball go to third base*. The plate umpire gets about three-fourths of the way up to third base in foul territory. If the ball and the runner both are going to be at third, then you go into the cutout at third base, telling your partner, "I got third," and take the play. If only one of the two things (ball or runner) is going to third base, don't go into fair territory, but stay foul; head back for home plate, telling your partner, "I'm going home." If you go into the cutout at third base for a play at third base and the ball gets by the fielder, break toward home, staying to the fair

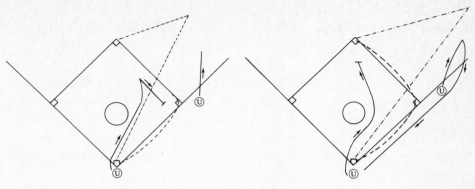

Single to right (nobody on base)   *Double to right (nobody on base)*

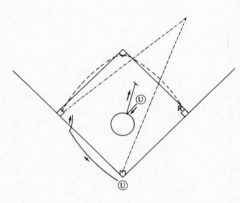

Runner first to third

side of the third-base line. This for the plate umpire is the same as an overthrow at second for the base umpire on a steal play. The most important things to remember are let your partner know where you are and watch the ball.

Double-play attempts

The field umpire should be ready to cover a double-play attempt before the batter even hits the ball. Knowing where you should be under different circumstances wil enable you to see the whole play.

Step forward once and turn with the batted ball as it bounces to the infielder. Watch the infielder handle the ball and make his throw. Second base is the most important part of the play. Watch the fielder take the ball there, and make sure he is holding the ball and stepping on the bag before he makes the pivot to first base. As soon as you see that play *completed* at second base, turn with the ball while making your call and then get set for the play at first base.

The toughest thing for umpires on this play is leaning in the right direction. To make sure you aren't moving toward second base at the time of the play at first base, or vice versa, turn like a soldier during drills. You must almost spin around when you're calling this play. When you spin take a couple of steps toward the play and get in the set position.

On all plays, get as close to a ninety-degree-angle view as possible.

The plate umpire should move toward third base for a possible subsequent play, especially when there is a runner on second as well as on first. The plate umpire should stay at home plate, though, when there's a man on third base.

The reverse double play

When the batter hits the ball to an inexperienced or uncertain first baseman in a double-play situation, the first baseman will often go directly to first base for the sure out, and then throw to second base to try to pickoff the lead runner. If you don't anticipate that play, you're likely to find youself running to the wrong base.

Don't move too close to first base to watch the play on the batter-runner. That play, after all, isn't going to be close unless the fielder suddenly drops the ball. As soon as you see that the first baseman is going to make the easy play, cheat a little and move toward second base. As soon as he completes the play at first, make a quick call as you're on the move to second base.

Get as close as possible to second base to watch the play. Get almost directly in front of the bag, shading a bit to first base. This play is going to be close, and, since the runner is trying to get into scoring position, important. Don't worry about the play exploding on you. It's just you and the infielder and base runner. The runner will try to elude the fielder, and the fielder might be off balance, so it's important for you to be right on top of the play.

Tag plays

The field umpire is responsible for all runners tagging up

at first and second base. The plate umpire is responsible for tag ups at third base.

When the ball is hit to right field, go to the edge of the infield grass just to the left of second base. Line up the runner and outfielder so you can see them both at the same time. Check the runner at first base; if he was tagging up and is very close to the bag, give him the benefit of the doubt.

If a ball is hit to left field and a runner is on second base, line up the runner and outfielder making the play, this time from the right side of second base. Quickly turn your attention toward a runner at first base by dropping back toward the mound.

The rest of the field umpire's movement—as well as the plate umpire's movement down toward third base—is the same as when a runner attempts to move from first to third base.

When the bases are loaded, the field umpire should move to the third-base side of the mound, then get into the set position to watch the outfield catch and the runners at first and second base. The plate umpire should move about halfway down the third-base line—about twenty to twenty-five feet into foul territory—to cover both the tag up at third base and a possible play at the plate.

The three-man and four-man systems

When a league's playoffs begin, officials of amateur leagues pay more attention to all aspects of the games, from concessions to attendance to umpires. Because the games mean so much to the participants, many leagues hire one or two extra umpires to make sure that all plays get good coverage.

If the umpires are not prepared for the three-man and four-man umpiring systms, those systems could, paradoxically, lead to poorer coverage of plays. Over the course of the regular season, the umpires get so accustomed to working with the two-man system that they are uncertain about where they should be when they have extra help.

Umpires who work with an extra umpire or two must resist the temptation to think their job will be easier. The idea behind hiring extra umpires is to increase play coverage, not reduce the workloads of the umpires. If the umpires ease up on a three- or four-man system, they could find themselves poorly positioned to make important calls.

When the league expands umpiring crews for playoff or all-star games, the umpires should meet well before the game to review the way they plan to cover plays. They probably should use one formal system rather than depend on their own instincts.

The three-man system enables you to cover the field more thoroughly. The most helpful points are: the pickoff at first, the double play, fair or foul down the third-base line, and covering trap balls in the outfield.

The following is a short list of mechanics for the three-man system:

1. On every batted ball, the third-base umpire moves to second base, then returns to third base after an out.

2. With second base open, the first-base umpire always remains at first base ready for the pickoff play. With two outs, runners at first and third, the first-base umpire stays at first and the third-base umpire stays in the infield.

3. If there's a possible double play (runner at first, runners at first and second, bases loaded), the third-base umpire is *always* in the infield, and the first-base umpire re-

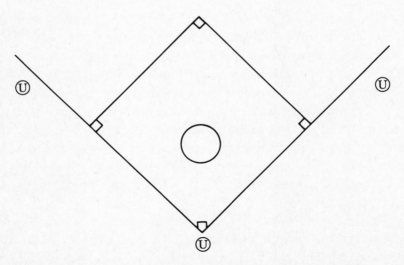

The umpires' positions under a three-man system.

mains at first base ready for the hard part of any double play.

4. If the third-base umpire goes into the outfield for a fair-foul, catch-no-catch play, he *never* returns: the crew then operates as if there were only two umpires.
5. The umpires rotate clockwise, the third-base umpire covering second, plate umpire covering third, and first-base umpire covering plate.
6. If the first-base umpire goes down the line in right field, he must return in foul ground, ready to cover any play at the plate.

Under a four-man system, the second-base umpire works behind second base on the outfield grass with no one on base. The second-base umpire works inside second base any time there is a possible force play or double play at second base.

The area each umpire will cover should be clear by the umpires' positions at the beginning of the play. When a field umpire has to move to the outfield, the remaining umpires will cover the infield area as they would under the three-man system.

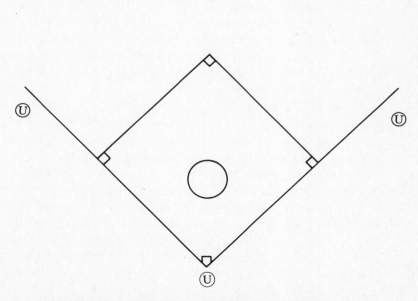

The umpires' positions under a four-man system.

The one-man system

All organized leagues should try to avoid using only one umpire in a game. Good two-, three-, and four-man crews will sometimes find themselves in poor position because of the nature of the play. Teams should understand that in working a one-man system, it is impossible to have good coverage on the field. The whole complexion of the game changes with one umpire.

On occasion, a two-man crew will be assigned to call a game but only one umpire will show up or one umpire will become injured during the game and will not be able to continue to work.

When only one umpire is available because of some kind of emergency, that umpire should offer the two teams three courses of action:

- Postpone the game until two umpires are available to work. Some leagues prefer to reschedule the game, especially when the game involves pennant contenders. But many leagues also have a difficult time finding a time and place to play makeup games. Ask your league officials whether this is the best approach.

- Get a volunteer from the crowd to work as a field umpire. If you do this, the proper umpire should work behind the plate. A five- or ten-minute briefing on the field umpire's job is in order. The umpire replacement should be deeply aware that he should act impartially. The experienced umpire should work with the field umpire throughout the game, telling him where to position himself to make calls.

- Have the lone umpire work the game by himself. In this case, he should stand behind the plate throughout the game. From this position, he can not only see all the pitches well, but can also see the balls hit down the first and third baselines. Ball-strike calls are always the toughest for any umpire because the difference between them can be so slight; they are also important because they set the pace of the game. The fair-foul calls often determine extra-base hits. By working behind the plate, the umpire can get down the field to cover plays at first and third. The only play for which the umpire won't be in good position will be at second base. All the umpire can do is make the other calls right and do his best at second.

EIGHT
Tough Plays

When umpires gather to talk about baseball, the conversation inevitably turns to the kinds of decisions umpires hate to face on the ball field. And when the umpires discuss those tough plays, there is an inevitable chorus: "I know one thing: when that play happens, I hope I'm someplace else."

An extreme example of such a play, of course, is the great pine tar controversy that my umpiring crew faced in Yankee Stadium in 1983, in which a home run by George Brett of the Kansas City Royals was nullified because Brett used too much pine tar on his bat. We had no way to win with our call: to take away Brett's home run did not seem just, but to ignore Brett's illegal bat would have been an arrogant snubbing of the official baseball rules.

Just thinking about that game sets off a voice in the back of my head: *When that play happens, I just hope I'm in Detroit.* I wish I *had* been in Detroit at the time. Or Cleveland. Or on vacation in the Caribbean. Or home sick in St. Petersburg.

The Pine Tar Game was a pure rules dispute. Rules disputes often present the knottiest problems because of contradicting, vague, or nonexistent rules. Everything that happens in a baseball game should be covered by the rulebook, but sometimes you have to patch several rules together to cover a complex situation. Stringing rules together often is a formula for disaster. That's what happened to us in the Pine Tar Game.

But baseball is full of other tough calls. Even in plays covered explicitly in the rulebook, such as the balk, the umpire is often in a damned-if-you-do-and-damned-if-you-don't position. If the umpire anticipates the play and gets in the right position, however, the problems that can come with these plays practically disappear.

And now, on to the toughest plays you will ever have to cover (again and again) on the field. . . .

Balks

A balk occurs when a pitcher misleads either the batter or the runner about whether he plans to pitch the ball or try to pick a runner off a base. The pitcher also commits a balk when he drops the ball while in contact with the rubber. Another balk is if the pitcher is on or straddling the rubber, without the ball, as in the "hidden ball trick."

There can be no balk without base runners.

The penalty for the balk is a one-base advance for the base runners. Once the balk occurs, the ball is dead unless the balk is on the pitch or the throw. On the pitched ball, if the batter and all runners advance one base, the balk is ignored. On the throw, if all runners advance, the ball remains alive.

The umpires should call the balk as soon as it happens so the pitcher can hold on to the ball and avoid hurting himself further by throwing the ball away or serving the hitter a fat pitch. When one umpire calls the balk, the other umpire should motion right away that he concurs. The balk is such a controversial play that the umpires need each other's support.

There are several ways for umpires to spot a balk. The umpires should watch the pitcher's legs, arms, and shoulders. If those body parts indicate a move toward home plate and the pitcher actually throws to a base, it's a balk. If those body parts indicate a move toward a base and the pitcher throws a pitch, it's a balk.

The balk call is really a matter of judging whether the pitcher unfairly fooled the batter or runner with his delivery. If the pitcher wants to pitch, he must bring his body forward toward the plate. If he wants to attempt a pickoff, he has to move his body in the direction of the base he's throwing to. There are a few key questions to ask in a balk situation. Did the pitcher break his motion? Did he start his pitch with only part of his foot in contact with the rubber? Did the pitcher fail to "step ahead" of the pitch? Did he take his hand off the pitch after starting his motion?

Both umpires may call a balk. Only the plate umpire, however, should make the call on the basis of what the pitcher does with his leg. There's no way for the field umpire to get a good angle on the pitcher's leg.

During the 1978 spring training games in Florida and Arizona, the major leagues experimented with chalk balk-lines on the pitcher's mound as a way of helping the umpires determine whether a pitcher balked. The lines were put down at a ninety-degree angle generating at the center. If the pitcher stepped outside the lines when he threw home, or if he stepped inside the lines when he attempted a pickoff, it was a balk.

Everybody thought those balk-lines properly marked what a pitcher could and could not do legally. But the lines did not last into the regular season games. Because pitchers work from different parts of the rubber—which is two feet long and six inches wide—pitchers land on different parts of the mound after they deliver the ball. The balk-lines ended up discriminating against some pitchers on the basis of what part of the rubber they worked from. The balk calls against pitchers who made the same pickoff moves but worked from different parts of the rubber varied.

Checked swing

The television instant replay has affected no single call more than the checked swing.

Replays of batters trying to abort their swings have led to great discussions—and confusion. Some say a batter swings when it appears that he *meant* to swing. Others say the test is whether he snaps his wrist on the swing. Others say the bat barrel must cross home plate, or part of the plate, for the umpire to call a strike. Still others say it's the batter's body that matters: if the batter takes a full stride, it's a swing.

For years, professional umpires tried to follow the first rule. Baseball is such a high-speed game—a pitch takes only half a second to go from the pitcher's hand to the plate, and the batter generally takes about a quarter of a second to swing his bat—that making such a judgment seemed to be the only practical approach. For years, players accepted the standard. Everyone on the field seemed to trust this instinctive approach to the problem.

And then came the instant replay. On the same pitch that everyone in the ballpark knew the batter did not mean to swing, the baseball broadcaster decided to take a second look. The cameras often showed that the batter came across the plate with his bat. Sure, he *meant* to stop his swing, but he didn't. "They should have called that a strike, Tony," the announcer intoned. Millions of fans who watched games on television, as well as players who see games on a clubhouse TV or instant-replay machine, began to demand that the call be made on the basis of what actually happened to the bat rather than what the batter *meant* to do.

Gone forever was the emphasis on intention.

The plate umpire should probably combine the two criteria when making the checked-swing call. You might discuss the problem with other umpires before the game.

On particularly close calls, the umpire can get help from his partner on the field if he is blocked out or calls a ball and the catcher asks for a second opinion. If the field umpire says it was a strike, change the call.

Infield fly rule

The infield fly rule is a frequent headache for umpires, especially umpires in amateur leagues.

Without the rule, the offensive team would be placed in a difficult situation whenever a batter hit a pop fly with base runners and fewer than two outs. The runner couldn't stray too far from his base, lest an infielder catch the ball and double him off his original base. And he couldn't stay too close to the base, lest the infielder intentionally allow the ball to fall to the ground and then turn a double play as if the batter had hit a ground ball.

The infield fly rule is outlined in Chapter 9's discussion of rules.

Tag plays

The tag play is one of the most exciting in all of baseball. If you get in the right position and concentrate, you should have no trouble getting the call right.

When you muff a tag play, the course of the game could change drastically. Just ask the 1970 Cincinnati Reds. The Baltimore Orioles easily beat the Reds in the World Series in five games. To this day, Manager Sparky Anderson says the Series's turning point was a play at the plate in which Baltimore catcher Elrod Hendricks tagged out Cincinnati outfielder Bernie Carbo at the plate. The umpire called Carbo out even though Hendricks didn't have the ball in his tagging hand. The umpire missed the play because his back was turned.

The most important thing to remember is to forget what you learned about covering the putout at first base. Forget about standing back to see the play. Get your nose in there as close as you can to watch a tag play. The play at first base is little more than a race between the runner and the ball. You just have to see who wins the race. Tag plays involve not only that bang-bang race, but also the skill, daring, timing, and fakery of the fielder and the runner.

Unless you get into the set position within six to eight feet from the play, you won't be able to see what happens. Watch the fielder get the ball and apply the tag. Make sure you know what

Stick your nose in those tag plays also. Make sure you can see all the participants in the play; don't be afraid to get too close.

part of the runner's body the fielder touches—and when. Make sure the fielder has complete control of the ball throughout the tag. The fielder must have possession of the ball when he comes away from the play.

Try to frame the complete picture, with the fielder on one side and the runner on the other. Know where the ball is in this picture.

Try to look between the fielder's glove hand and the runner so you can get a good angle on the tag. If you connect the glove and the runner with an imaginary line, your position should form a right angle with the play. If the runner slides away from the tag and all three of you are in a straight line, you're going to have a tough time seeing the tag.

When the play is over, stay with the action. The base runner could overslide the base. If the runner is off the base for even a split second and the fielder tags him, he's out. If the outcome of the play changes because of a fumbled ball or an overslide, don't hesitate to change your call.

Make your call quickly and decisively. Let the whole world know what happened. On close plays, your decisiveness will dispel any uncertainty.

Continuous plays

Baseball fans call the play exciting. Managers say it's the kind of play that tells them the most about the players' instincts as fielders and base runners. Umpires sometimes wish the play would never develop.

The continuous play is the most difficult situation for the umpires in a two- or three-man system. As its moniker indicates, the play is a series of situations that develops from one pitch, throw, or batted ball. What happens in a continuous play is unpredictable and hellish for umpires.

For example, say two umpires are calling a game between the Mets and Padres. Mookie Wilson and Gary Carter are the Mets' base runners on first and third with one out. Pinch-hitter Rusty Staub hits a soft line drive to right field. Padre right fielder Tony Gwynne hustles in for the ball, but whether he catches the ball or merely traps it is questionable. There's one tough call (1). Gwynne throws the ball to catcher Terry Kennedy. The play at the plate is close, because Carter was hugging third base in the event that the ball would be caught. Another tough call (2). Kennedy then whirls and throws the ball to first base, where Staub is caught daydreaming. There's a rundown play—another tough play for the umpires (3). While that play is in progress, Wilson chugs around third base for home. Staub avoids the tag near first base, possibly running out of the baseline. Another tough call (4). The throw to the plate is wide, and Kennedy attempts to apply a swipe tag. Another call (5). Staub is now headed to second base (6). . . .

And so it goes. How are the umpires supposed to get into position for all of these calls? From the outset, the umpires work at a disadvantage because of the need to cover the outfield. The players act on the ball as if they were cushions in a pinball game. The umpires must change direction constantly to get to the plays. Is it futile?

Sometimes it might appear so. But if the umpires think ahead and visualize the diamond as a constantly shifting pattern, they can see almost every play well.

The key is that the plate and field umpires must stay in the

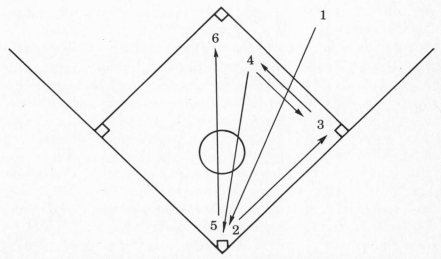

As you can see, the umpires in the hypothetical Mets–Padres game had to move all around the field to make all of the calls. At each point, the umpires should be asking themselves what can go wrong next. What can go wrong often does.

front and back parts of the diamond, respectively. Don't ever stray too much to one part of the diamond. Always be in the center of the diamond where you can spin quickly and see a play at a different part of the diamond.

Try to anticipate plays. Where are the base runners? Is the cutoff man doing his job? How fast are the fielders and runners? How daring are the runners? What are the coaches doing? How long will it take a player to retrieve a ball thrown into foul territory? Where are the fielders? Do the fielders leave any bases uncovered? Anticipating plays will help guide you through messy situations.

The rundown play

The offensive team has a runner on first base. The batter hits the ball into the right-field corner for a possible double. The right fielder grabs the ball and throws it to second base. But the shortstop, who takes the right fielder's throw, sees the lead runner overrun third base. Instead of making a play on the batter-runner, he fires to third base. The runner is caught between two infielders, who try to "run him down" with the ball.

The umpire is also caught in the play. And if he doesn't position himself correctly he could find himself in a pickle on a subsequent play.

Rundown plays occur when the base runner makes a mistake, when the pitcher picks a runner off a base, and when an outfielder or the infield cutoff man makes an exceptional play. Rundown plays upset the normal ebb and flow of a ballgame—usually when everyone on the field least expects the play.

The 1983 World Champion Baltimore Orioles' defense was famous for executing the rundown with one throw—in other words, they didn't allow the base runner to waste the fielders' precious time by forcing them to throw the ball back and forth. When, say, third baseman Todd Cruz got the ball after a base runner overran third base, he chased the runner until the runner was practically right on top of catcher Rick Dempsey. Then Cruz flipped the ball to Dempsey, who applied the easy tag. End of play.

Most big-league teams—not to mention college or other amateur-league teams—are not quite so skillful. Rundowns usually amount to two or more fielders sandwiching the base runner, throwing the ball back and forth to each other and eventually tagging—or missing—the runner. Those plays often are as difficult for the umpire as the players.

Be ahead of the runner. It isn't enough to be even with him, because you have to be as still as possible when the fielder attempts the tag.

If there are two umpires and the ball is at one end of the rundown, the umpire at the other end of the play should take a glance

The umpires should stand on opposite sides of the rundown play. Try to get ahead of the throws so you're not moving too much when the fielder applies the tag. When you're working the play alone, try to look down the line at the players.

at the rest of the field to see if something else is happening.

If there is only one base runner when a rundown develops, both umpires should cover the play. The umpires should get on opposite sides of the baseline and position themselves just between the runner and the fielder. Fielders involved in the rundown often are relieved during the play by a teammate; both umpires should remember this and know which fielders are involved with the play *at every moment*.

If there are other base runners besides the man caught in the rundown, only one umpire should devote his complete attention to the rundown. The other should move to a position where he can see other plays develop, and he should watch the rundown from that position. He should be ready to make a call on the rundown play, but he should also be ready to turn his attention elsewhere.

The umpires must communicate with each other on this play. If one umpire thinks he can handle the play on his own, he should yell: "I got it all—you cover third (or wherever another play might develop)." If the umpires are going to team up for the play, one should yell: "I got this end."

When both umpires are covering the play, make sure you know who's going to make the call. You don't want to both make calls at the same time—especially since the calls could be different. Before you make a call at the end of the play, make sure you establish quick eye contact with your partner. That's usually all it takes to communicate who should make the call. It is usually obvious which umpire has a better view.

Watch more than the simple chase play. Look for other possible calls—such as obstruction and offensive interference.

Think ahead. What will the base runners and fielders do if a fielder overthrows the ball? What if the ball goes into the stands? What part of the field will the action shift to after the play is executed? Be ready to get in position for the next play.

Time plays

Time plays are not situations that develop just before a midnight curfew or when the sun sets and the home team turns on the lights. They are not plays that have a time limit of forty-five seconds, and they are not plays that involve delay-of-game claims.

Time plays simply are those situations when the sequence

of events determines which events should count. They are the plays that often determine which team wins a game. If the umpire botches a time play, he invites the ire of the team that loses out.

The time play occurs when a base runner crosses home plate at about the same time that the defense records the third out of the inning. If a team scores a run *before the defense records the third out of the inning*, the run counts *unless* the third out came on a force play or the failure of the batter-runner to reach first safely.

Say two teams are tied 2–2 with two outs in the bottom of the eighth inning. There is a runner on second base for the home team when his teammate singles to left-center field. The batter-runner is thrown out trying to stretch the hit into a double. That's the third out of the inning. But the lead runner touches home plate before the batter-runner is tagged out—and the umpire rules that the run counts. The fielders complain that the run should not count, and they threaten to protest the call. Who's right?

The umpire is right, because he saw the base runner cross the plate before the third out of the inning. The manager cannot lodge a protest because the rules are clear. All anyone can complain about is the umpire's *judgment*. Ultimately, though, the umpire's judgment calls will stand.

This brings up an important point about the umpire's job in a time play. Time plays require both umpires to watch two or more plays that are happening at the same time. The umpires must know *what happens* and *when it happens*. As with the possible sacrifice fly ball, the umpire must watch the base runners and the fielders and know what happens and when.

Line up all of the relevant action during a time play, if possible. This is a play where you'll need to put your peripheral vision to work. You must get into a position where you can see two or three things happening at the same time.

Arguments

Nothing rouses players or fans quite as much as a good-old-fashioned-angrier-than-hell-did-you-even-*see*-that-play-ump? rhubarb.

The frustrated sputterings of a few players and coaches is a unique part of baseball at almost every level. I don't suppose arguments with umpires start as early as tee-ball competition, but arguments do occur in leagues with pretty young players—if not on-field arguing, then at least the bench jockeying of a few bad sports.

What to do with the arguers depends on what level you are umpiring. The umpire should make it clear to Little Leaguers that he will not accept any sniping. If a player complains about a call, the umpire should tell him to stop complaining and start playing ball immediately—and then tell the coach to put some reins on the argumentative youngster.

Youth leagues were established for boys and girls to learn baseball and softball in a competitive but well-mannered atmosphere. Players in those leagues are impressionable, and it is here that they should be taught not to imitate Billy Martin when they don't get what they want. These kids have to learn how to lose as well as win gracefully.

Often, the coach of the team or a parent is the problem. Deal with them politely but firmly. Tell them that you make the calls as best as possible, that you had the best view of the play, and it's time to play ball again.

The players and coaches usually are not chronic complainers until high-school ball, where the game becomes more serious. More people watch the games. The teams go to great expense to hold the games—and to pay the umpires. Sometimes a college scholarship or professional contract is on the line. The players devote hours and hours each week to drills and practice, and they have a greater emotional stake in the game.

When an argument develops, try to keep it one-on-one. Don't let the players and coaches gang up on you or your partner. If you find yourself overwhelmed, stand back, hold up your hands, and announce that you can only talk to one person at a time—and that person will be either the player involved or the manager.

Listen to the argument, especially if the play in question was particularly close. Don't say too much—let the upset parties do the talking. As President Calvin Coolidge once remarked, nobody can hold what you don't say against you. Just say something bland like: "I'm telling you, the tag beat the runner." And don't be afraid to repeat the statement: you won't earn points for your eloquence. Be polite but act as if you were bored with the argument. The out-

come, after all, is a foregone conclusion. Don't allow the player or coach to draw you into a complex discussion about the specifics of the play.

Your objective is to allow the aggrieved party to speak his mind, and then to get the game going again.

If your partner is engaged in an argument, don't get involved right away. It's his problem. But if the argument lasts more than a minute or two, stand nearby. Listen to what both sides are saying. As an outsider, free of the emotional fireworks, you might be able to step in to break it up. Ask what's wrong, and ask how you can help resume the game. Say something like: "OK, skipper, you've had your say, but we're here to play ball, so let's go."

If the manager is arguing a rule interpretation, do not hesitate to call your partner over for a private conference. I emphasize the word private. Then, if necessary, take out the rulebook and figure out exactly how to rule. If the manager's interpretation is correct, don't hesitate to rule in his favor. Whatever you do, explain your final decision with specific references to the rulebook.

A team may play a game under protest only if there are rules conflicts. The team must lodge the protest before the next play. Announce to the players and the fans that the team is playing the game under protest. And get the game going again.

What should you allow the arguer to say? Our approach in the big leagues is to allow them to say we made a horsebleep call, but not to say we personally are horsebleep. If the arguer gets personal, tell him he risks ejection. If he continues in a personal vein after one or two warnings, throw him out of the game.

What if he refuses to leave the field? Stay with him for a while, but give him increasingly stern warnings that he risks forfeit if he doesn't leave the field so that the game can continue. If he stays on the field five minutes after you tell him to leave, give him a final warning. Remind him that a forfeit is unfair to his team. If he continues to argue, forfeit the game. Remind him you're forfeiting the game with the authority vested in you by the league president—and that the coach will be hearing from the league president soon.

Trick plays

Baseball's many interesting strategies involve little duplicity or foul play.

As the gentleman's game of America, baseball demands that its teams respect one another. The Official Baseball Rules prohibit the defense from doctoring baseballs, throwing pitches at the batter, or distracting the batter by running in his field of vision. The rules also prohibit either team from physically getting in the opposition's way or verbally taunting opposing players.

The umpire does not need to follow the game's inside strategies, but he does need to watch out for an occasional favorite of all managers—the hidden-ball trick. It's a play in which a fielder pretends he doesn't have the ball and, when the base runner least expects it, surprises him by tagging him out.

You must know two facts when a team attempts a hidden-ball trick: Who has the ball? Is the ball alive or dead? If you know those facts and keep an eye on the players you are responsible for watching, you'll be OK.

There are a few other trick plays.

Pat Corrales, who has managed the Philadelphia Phillies and

Cleveland Indians, pulls one favorite trick play about three times a year. I was involved in one such play in an Indians–Baltimore Orioles game.

The Tribe had runners on first and third. Brett Butler, the runner on first, fell down at first, accidentally-on-purpose. Orioles catcher Rick Dempsey, eager to nail Butler, fell down in anticipation of the pitch—and the pitch went sailing all the way to the backstop. The runner from third scored. By following the orders of Corrales to fall down, Butler ruined Dempsey's concentration.

Rickey Henderson of the New York Yankees also likes to trick the opposition. After sprinting down the line, he stops after reaching first base—and, just when the pitcher and umpire least expect it, he darts to second base for a steal.

The main thing to remember is to watch the game like an umpire, not like a spectator. Always think ahead to the next play or set of plays. When one player does something that attracts everyone's attention, keep an eye on the rest of the players on the field—they might use the distraction to their advantage.

I know of one case where the umpire was actually part of a trick play—and his role in the play got the game going faster. John Rice, the veteran umpire who helped break me into the big leagues, worked some Red Sox games where Jimmy Piersall was up to crazy tricks. Piersall never liked to play the second game of a double-header, so early in the second game he'd throw a fit over the most obvious ball-strike calls—just to get ejected from the game. One day his manager, Jimmy Dyckes, asked umpire Rice to tell Piersall: "Look, Jimmy, I know you just want to go home. But I'm not going to throw you out of the game, so settle down and let's get the game over with."

Sure enough, Piersall had a fit over a routine strike call. Rice told Piersall he wasn't going to eject him no matter how violent he got. True to Dyckes's prediction, Piersall settled down. He never again interrupted a game with his ridiculous act just to get ejected.

Overthrows

When a fielder throws a ball away, the umpire needs to adjust. He must have a complete command of the rules governing overthrows. If the ball gets stuck in a fence, what happens to the runners? What if a fan grabs a ball that has bounded into foul territory? What if an umpire boots the ball while it's in foul territory? When is the ball dead, and when is it alive? In general, what are runners entitled to automatically, and what are their limits?

All these questions are answered in Chapter 9's discussion of rules.

Once you know the rules, everything else is easy. Just know where the base runners are at the start of the play and at the time of the overthrow. Know the flow of the play. Know the bases where a play is likely to develop (usually second base) and the bases where a play is not likely to develop (usually first base).

Most of all, know where the ball is. Nothing can happen without a ball.

NINE
The Rulebook Made Easy

For even the most baseball-crazy person, the baseball rulebook is one of the most boring books ever published. It is probably the most vital part of baseball literature, but I would not expect to see someone curl up with the book like he would with a good suspense novel. The rules are arranged not according to the situations that develop in games, but according to the game's objectives and major participants. Here's the breakdown of the rulebook:

Section 1: Objectives of the Game
Section 2: Definitions of Terms
Section 3: Game Preliminaries
Section 4: Starting and Ending a Game
Section 5: Putting the Ball into Play . . . Live Ball
Section 6: The Batter
Section 7: The Runner
Section 8: The Pitcher
Section 9: The Umpire
Section 10: The Official Scorer

Every umpire should know the rules as well as a mechanic knows the parts of an engine. If an umpire doesn't know even the most arcane rules, he will not earn the respect he needs to control games throughout the season.

Nick Bremigan, an American League umpire who teaches at my umpire school in Florida, is probably the leading rules guru in the major leagues. Bremigan has rearranged the rules so they are more relevant to game situations. A former high-school physical education and social studies teacher, Bremigan calls his system "Rules for Idiots." The system covers practically all plays an umpire could be confronted with during a game.

Simply reading a set of rules isn't going to make an umpire an expert in dealing with sticky rules disputes. Only experience can make someone into an excellent rules umpire. I tell my students to do exactly what Bremigan and I do to keep our knowledge of rules fresh: Any time you are involved in a play involving a difficult rule, write a short reminder of the situation near the appropriate rule in your rulebook. Whenever you have a few idle minutes, look over those notes.

All organized leagues—from Little League to the Japanese professional leagues—use the same set of rules. They are divided into the ten sections listed above, and the breakdown is the same for all leagues. Rule 6.02 will be the same for a Little League game in Huntington, Long Island, a Yomiuri Giants game in Tokyo, and a Los Angeles Dodgers game in California. The only time baseball leagues differ in their rules is when a league adopts an extra rule, such as Little League Baseball's requirement that base runners touch a base until a pitch is made.

Get a copy of the Official Baseball Rulebook and take it to every game you umpire. The book is updated annually by the major leagues and published by *The Sporting News*. Also get a listing of the rule differences for the leagues you work in.

The following explanation of the rules—based mostly on Nick Bremigan's "Rules for Idiots"—includes references to the rule numbers. Also included is a list of some of the most important rule differences of major amateur leagues in the United States.

I. Playing conditions

The umpires' role. The umpires have the full authority of the league president during a game. The plate umpire is known as the umpire-in-chief, or the crew chief. Once the game begins, the crew chief has final say on rules disputes, field conditions, spectators; and disputes with players, coaches, and managers. In a situation that is not covered explicitly by the rulebook, the crew chief will have authority to determine how to deal with it. The authority is broad. Joe West, a National League umpire, once ejected a camera crew in Shea Stadium for showing a replay of a controversial play in the Mets' dugout. When the umpires disagree about a rule interpretation, the crew chief will make the final decision. [Rule 9.04 (c)]

Visits to mound.   A manager or coach may go to the mound twice in an inning—but the second visit will automatically result in the pitcher's removal from the game. The manager or coach may not make two visits to the mound during one man's plate appearance. [Rule 8.06]

Lights.   The umpire-in-chief has authority to order the lights turned on whenever he considers them necessary. [Rule 4.14]

Ejections.   Any umpire has authority to order a player, coach, team or stadium employee, or fan to leave the ballpark. A Pacific Coast League umpire went so far as to eject a bat boy in 1984 for refusing to obey his instructions to move some equipment off the field. Ejected team members or officials must be "well removed" from the playing field. [Rule 4.07]

Coaches.   Each team must station two uniformed coaches on the playing field along the two baselines. Those coaches should stand in coaches boxes by first and third base. [Rule 4.05]

Equipment and game setting.   See Rule 1 in the official rulebook for regulations concerning the playing field, bases, rubber, bats, balls, dugouts, gloves, helmets, uniforms, lineups, and rosters.

Game delays, postponements, cancellations, forfeits.   Regulations for the games that do not run their full course, for whatever reason, vary greatly from league to league.

II. Gentlemen's rules

Roger Angell, the baseball writer for *The New Yorker*, has noted that baseball differs from other sports in one major way. In most sports, the athletes spend most of their time chasing or trying to defend one person who has possession of the ball; in baseball, the players act on the ball individually. Each player is given the opportunity to do what he can with the ball—without an inordinate amount of distraction from his opponents. Several rules are designed to protect the players from unnecessary distractions. These are the gentlemen's rules:

The beanball.   The most important of the gentlemen's rules is the prohibition against throwing the ball at a batter. When the umpire thinks a pitcher has thrown a beanball, the umpire should give a formal warning to the pitcher and his manager, as well as the manager of the opposing team. If the umpire believes that the pitcher for either team throws a second beanball, he should eject the pitcher from the game immediately.

Some people claim the beanball has a place in baseball because of its wide acceptance for so many years. These people say it's part of the game. As *Sports Illustrated* pointed out a few years ago, a lot of other practices that were once part of the game—like bigotry, spitballs, and spiking—have finally been rejected. Just because these things were once accepted doesn't make them right. [Rule 8.02 (d)]

Harassment.   A gentlemen's rule with a spotty history of enforcement is the prohibition of harassment of opponents. No member of a team—from the manager and players all the way down to the bat boy—may try to incite a demonstration of spectators that would disrupt the game. Players and coaches may not shout anything such as "Time!" to an opposing pitcher that would make him commit a balk. Team members also are prohibited from saying anything to an umpire, spectator, or opposing player that insults their personality. No one is permitted to make intentional contact with an umpire.

In professional baseball, this is a tough one to enforce. So much of baseball lore is tied up in the needling of the opposition, and it's sometimes hard to figure out whether that needling is good- or ill-natured. When he managed the San Francisco Giants, Frank Robinson caused a stir by making hand motions to his nose when an opposing pitcher with a history of cocaine addiction was on the mound. There's no need for that kind of personal insult. When you're uncertain about whether to apply this rule, you should probably give the players or manager in question a warning that they might violate this rule. People who do violate the rule should be ejected from the game. [Rule 4.06 (a)]

Distracting the batter.   Fielders are not allowed to distract the batter by deliberately running in his field of vision. Because hitting can be dangerous, the batter must be allowed to concentrate. If a fielder moves around the middle of the diamond with the obvious intent of distracting the batter, he should be ejected. [Rule 4.06 (b)]

Harassing the umpire. When a team's bench shows violent disapproval of the umpire's calls, the umpire may order the player who is causing the trouble to leave the bench for the clubhouse. If the umpire cannot determine which player or coach is to blame, he can order all coaches and substitute players to leave the bench and to reappear only when they are inserted into the game. [Rule 4.08]

Delay of game. Players attempt to delay a game for two major reasons.

When the weather is bad, the losing team often delays in an attempt to avoid completion of the minimum number of innings for an official game. Five innings constitute a complete game in the major leagues; when rain threatens completion of the full nine innings, the losing team often stalls with the hope that the game will be halted before the end of five innings.

Teams also stall to allow a teammate—usually a pitcher—to get prepared to enter the game. If a team's pitcher is getting pounded and a relief pitcher is not ready to enter the game, the beleaguered pitcher's teammates will find any excuse to stall. They will hold conferences on the mound; they will pretend they have lost their contact lenses; they will pretend they don't understand their manager's signals.

If such delays seriously interrupt a game, the umpire should forfeit the game to the opponent only as a last resort. [Rule 4.15 (a-d, g)] The umpires can also forfeit a game to the visiting team if the home team's grounds crew does not comply with orders. [Rule 4.16]

When the pitcher delays a game, the umpire should call a ball if there are no base runners or a balk if there are base runners. [Rules 8.04, 8.05 (h)] The pitcher also faces ejection from the game if he delays the game by throwing the ball to teammates without attempting to retire a runner. [Rule 8.02 (c)]

When fielders delay a game by throwing the ball to each other for no reason, the umpire should forfeit the game to the opponent if, after warning, you receive no cooperation. [Rule 4.15 (b)]

In an attempt to rattle the pitcher, batters sometimes spend too much time preparing to step into the batter's box. When an umpire suspects a delay by the batter, he should instruct the pitcher to throw pitches—and make "strike" calls for every pitch for which the batter is not properly set in the box. [Rule 6.02 (c)]

Fortunately, the simple threat to call a strike or ball or to forfeit the game usually is enough to get the players going. But there will be times when you need to play your ace card. Umpire Marty Springstead once forfeited a Baltimore Orioles game when Manager Earl Weaver refused to order his players to take their positions after a controversial call.

III. The runner

Base runners are expected to run directly to each of the bases until they are put out by the defense. The runners must move around the bases in the order in which they bat in the lineup, within the baselines, without overrunning or oversliding the bases, and without interfering with the defensive players.

The base runner is allowed to overrun or overslide only first base. When a batter-runner runs to first base, he may run past the bag down the right-field line; but if he does not return directly to the bag—if he starts toward second base, for example—he is liable to be put out. Any time a runner runs or slides past second or third base, he is liable to be put out by a fielder. [Rule 7.08 (c,j)]

When one base runner passes one of his teammates on the basepaths, the runner who is too far along should be called out. When two runners are standing on the same base, the second runner should be called out when he is tagged by a fielder and the first runner should be entitled to the base. These are time plays, so the timing of the base running infraction could affect other plays happening during the same set of plays. [Rules 7.08 (h) and 7.03]

The batter-runner should be called out for running out of the baseline when he runs more than three feet to one side of the line *and* interferes with a fielder taking the throw at first base. He will not be called out if he was merely trying to get out of the fielder's way. [Rule 6.05 (k)] The batter-runner can also be called out for running out of the baseline if he leaves the baseline and "obviously abandon[s] his effort to touch the next base." [Rule 7.08 (a)(2)]

Other base runners should also be called out for running more than three feet outside the baselines—unless trying to avoid interfering with the fielder's play. This happens when the runner is trying to elude a tag. [Rule 7.08 (a)(1)]

IV. Pitcher infractions

Here are several rules the umpire should keep in mind concerning the pitchers:

Doctored pitches. From baseball's earliest years, pitchers have attempted to gain an advantage on batters by slightly defacing the baseball. The baseball is such a small object that any changes could drastically affect what the air does to the ball as it hurtles toward the batter. Doctored baseballs look like ordinary pitches until the last minute, when the ball dives in or away from the helpless batter. Because the spitball, as the pitch generally is called, is so difficult to hit (not to mention dangerous), the lords of baseball outlawed the pitch in 1920.

Despite the ban, pitchers have continued to throw illegal pitches. They have used petroleum jelly, dirt, thumbtacks, knives, and, of course, good old-fashioned human saliva, to turn pitches into dancers. The umpire's job is to prevent the pitcher from getting this illegal edge on hitters.

The umpire should warn the pitcher not to throw the spitter if he suspects the pitcher is throwing it. If the umpire thinks the pitcher throws a spitter on a subsequent pitch, he should eject the pitcher from the game. [Rules 3.02, 8.02 (a,b)]

Illegal pitches. The pitcher throws an illegal pitch when:

* he "quick-pitches" the ball, or gives the batter and umpire insufficient time to prepare for the pitch. [Rules 2.00, 3.02, 8.01 (d), 8.05 (e)]
* he fails to touch the rubber with his pivot foot while pitching the ball. [Rules 2.00, 8.01 (a,b,d,e)]

To prevent the pitcher from pitching closer to home plate, the rules require the pitcher to touch the pitching rubber while making his pitch. The right-handed pitcher should push off the rubber with his right foot; the left-hander should push off with his left foot.

If the pitcher does not touch the rubber when he throws the ball, the umpire should call a balk if there are base runners or a ball if there are no base runners.

V. Force plays

A force play occurs when a runner has no place to go except a specific base—when the runner is literally forced by another runner to vacate his original base and attempt to reach the next base. A force play can occur only when the batter becomes a runner. [Rule 2.00 force play]

If there is a runner on first base and the batter hits a ground ball, the runner has no place to go except second base—because the batter has become a runner and has to go to first base. If a fielder who is holding the ball touches second base, that runner is out. The fielder does not need to tag the runner.

The fielder is allowed to tag the runner with the ball rather than step on the base if he chooses.

A force play is removed on all runners who have advanced farther than another runner who is forced out. [Rule 7.08 (e)]

Suppose the Yankees' Dale Berra is on second base and Dave Winfield is on first base. If Winfield is forced out at second base on a Don Mattingly ground ball, Berra cannot be forced out anymore. Or if Mattingly is retired on a ground ball or pop fly, Berra and Winfield cannot be forced out at third and second anymore.

The force play is removed as soon as the batter-runner is retired. A force play does not exist when no runners precede the runner in question.

VI. Catch or no-catch

When a fielder makes a difficult play on a fly ball, there frequently is a question about whether or not the fielder actually catches the ball. There are a few simple rules to follow on the catch-no-catch call.

Some people think that a player has caught the ball as soon as he grabs it. That's how it works in football, but not in baseball. The fielder must have secure possession and complete control of the ball for the umpire to rule that the ball was caught. If the player releases the ball, it must be a *voluntary* release. If a fielder drops the ball as the result of a collision or fall, he has not caught the ball. The fielder also cannot catch the ball after it touches the fence, umpire, or an offensive player.

If the fielder drops the ball while in the process of throwing, it's still a catch because the player was starting his next action after the catch. [Rule 2.00 catch]

VII. Foul tips and foul balls (Rule 2.00)

A foul tip is a ball hit sharply and directly from the bat to the catcher's glove or hand and is caught by the catcher.

A foul ball is any nontip that is batted into foul territory. Foul balls can be caught for outs regardless of the count on the batter. If the batter hits a line drive that lands outside of the left field or right field line, it's a foul. If a batter hits a ball back to the catcher that has a slight arc, it's a foul ball. If the batter hits a ball straight back to the catcher's mask, it's a foul ball.

The distinction between the foul tip and the foul ball is important for several reasons.

First of all, a foul tip is live, while a foul ball is usually dead. The only time the runner can advance on a foul ball is when a fielder catches that ball; in that case, the runner must tag up before attempting to move to the next base. Base runners may not attempt to move to the next base when a fielder misses a foul ball, but they can try to advance on any foul tip.

Of course, because the ball is always alive on a foul tip, the base runner is more vulnerable than he would be on a foul ball. If he is caught snoozing off the base, he can be thrown out by the catcher.

The foul tip/foul ball distinction is also important because a foul tip can be only a strike. The only way a batter can be called out on a foul tip is when that foul tip is the third strike; even then, the catcher must catch the ball for the batter to complete the strikeout. A foul ball that is caught, however, is a putout.

The importance of the foul tip call is simple enough. But actually making the call is sometimes hard because many managers and players do not really know the difference between a foul tip and a foul ball. They often argue that a ball is a foul tip unless it rises, say, higher than the catcher's head. The umpire must be able to explain that only a batted ball that goes *straight back* to the catcher's hands is a foul tip.

Other problems for umpires develop when the catcher does not handle the ball cleanly on a foul-tip third strike. For the umpire to call the third strike, the ball must first hit the catcher's hand or glove. The catcher can bobble the ball and then catch it for a third strike, but he cannot catch the ball off his chest, mask, or shin guards for a third strike.

VIII. Time plays

Time plays develop when a base runner crosses home plate at about the same time that the defense records the third out of the inning. If a team scores a run *before the defense records the third out of the inning*, that run counts unless the inning's third out came on a force play. No run can score when the third out comes on a force play. [Rules 2.00, 4.09 (a), 7.08 (g), 7.10 (notes), 7.12]

For example, say the Atlanta Braves and Los Angeles Dodgers are tied 2–2 with two outs in the bottom of the eighth inning at Dodger Stadium. Steve Sax of the Dodgers is on second base when Mike Marshall singles to left-center field. Marshall is thrown out trying to stretch the hit into a double. Sax touches home plate before Marshall is tagged out, so the run counts.

IX. Option plays

Every once in a while, a manager can put himself in the umpire's position and determine the outcome of a play. The so-called "option play" occurs when a player on one team does something illegal during a play, and that illegal action affects the performance of a player from the opposing team.

When the option play develops, the manager of the second team—the team that was put at a disadvantage by the illegal action—can either accept the end result of the play or appeal the play to the umpire and have the penalty evoked. The smart decision is usually apparent.

What happens during these option plays is that one team does something illegal, which might put the other team at a disadvantage, but the other team completes the play anyway.

There are three ways that an option play can develop:

(1) The catcher interferes with the batter's swing, but the batter hits the ball anyway. [Rule 6.08 (c)]

(2) A defensive team records three outs and therefore ends the inning, but during the play that results in the third out the hitter or base runners do something illegal and the other team appeals. [Rules 4.09 (a) and 7.10]

(3) A pitcher throws an illegal pitch, but the batter hits the ball anyway. [Rules 8.01 (d) and 8.02 (c)]

X. Dead ball, live ball

There are three kinds of baseballs: live ball, immediate dead ball, and delayed dead ball. If the umpire does not know what distinguishes the three kinds of balls, he can put a team at a disadvantage at a crucial point in a game.

A live ball, of course, is any ball that is in play. When the ball is alive, the base runners may attempt to get to the next base, the batter can attempt to swing at pitches, and the defense can attempt to retire its opponents. A ball is alive almost the entire game. [Rules 2.00, 5.09 (a-h), 6.05 (g), 6.09 (d,e,f,g,h), 7.05 (a, f-i), 7.06 (a)]

An immediate dead ball is the ball at any point in the game when no plays are permitted to take place. If a fielder misses a pop fly in foul territory, the ball is immediately dead. Nothing can happen until the umpire declares the ball to be live again.

A delayed dead ball is a ball that is about to be dead. Delayed dead ball plays occur when a player does something illegal during a play, but that illegal action does not prevent the play from being completed. The ball is not dead until the play ends.

Delayed dead ball situations. The umpire should call a delayed dead ball situation when:

- The catcher interferes with the batter's swing, but the batter still manages to hit the ball. [Rule 6.08 (c)]
- The batter interferes with a defensive player, but a play or throw follows the interference. [Rule 6.06 (c)]
- The plate umpire interferes with the catcher, but the catcher still makes a throw. [Rule 5.09 (b)]

- The pitcher balks, but still throws or pitches the ball. [Rule 8.05 Pen]
- A defensive player obstructs a base runner. [Rule 7.06 (b)]

When the umpire calls a delayed dead ball, he should compare the penalty for the illegal act with the situation that developed in the play. He should make sure the team hurt by the illegal play gets *at least* what it would have received had the play stopped right away.

Suppose the Houston Astros are playing the Atlanta Braves. Dale Murphy is the Braves' base runner, with Chris Chambliss at bat. The Astros' catcher, Jim Leeson, expects Murphy to run, so he leans forward on the next pitch—leans so far, in fact, that he interferes with Chambliss' swing. Chambliss still manages to hit the ball. If he flies out, he gets a free pass to first base because of the catcher's interference. If he gets a hit, his manager will have the choice of taking the catcher's interference award or the hit.

Dead ball, runners advance one base. The runners are permitted to advance one base when the ball is declared dead because:

- The ball gets stuck in the umpire's mask. [Rule 5.09 (g)]
- The pitcher throws the ball into dead territory while standing on the pitcher's rubber. [Rule 7.05 (h)]
- A fielder falls into dead territory after catching the ball [Rule 7.04 (c)]
- The pitch touches a runner who is attempting to score. [Rule 5.09 (h)]
- The pitcher balks but does not pitch or throw the ball. [Rule 8.05 Pen]
- A base runner attempts to steal on a pitch when there's a catcher's interference called. [Rule 7.04 (d)]

Dead ball, runners return. The umpire should call the ball dead and order the runners to return to the base where they were standing at the beginning of the pitch when:

- A foul ball is not caught. [Rule 5.09 (e)]
- There is an illegally batted ball. [Rule 5.09 (d)]
- The batter interferes with the catcher, unless the runner is thrown out. [Rule 6.06 (c)]
- The batter is called out for batting out of turn. [Rule 6.07 (b)]

Dead ball, runners return unless moved forward. The umpire should order the runners to return to their original base unless they move forward when:

- The runner interferes with the fielders. [Rule 7.09 (g)]
- A ball batted into fair territory strikes the runner or umpire. [Rule 5.09 (f)]
- A batter is hit with a pitch. [Rule 5.09 (a)]

XI. Batted ball hits a runner or umpire

The Chicago Cubs are playing the Pittsburgh Pirates. With the Cubs' Bob Dernier on second base and Ryne Sandberg on third, Jody Davis steps to the plate. Davis hits a ball that hits umpire Steve Rippley—who was headed to second base to cover a possible stolen base attempt—before Bucs' shortstop Alex Heard can field the ball. It would have been an easy play for Heard. Rippley calls time and puts Davis on first and the other two Cubs back at second and third. Pittsburgh manager Chuck Tanner complains because he wants the putout Heard surely would have made. And Chicago manager Jim Frey is upset because he wants Sandberg to be allowed to score. Did the umpire do the right thing? [Rules 2.00 interference, umpire; 5.09 (f); 6.09 (c)]

It might not seem fair to deny Heard a chance to field the ball or the Cubs a chance to score, but Rippley did the right thing. His decision was consistent with the often confusing rules that cover runners and umpires who are hit with a batted ball.

If the ball hits the runner or umpire *before* passing any fielder, except pitcher, the ball is declared dead, any runner hit with the ball is called out, the batter is awarded first base, and the runners return to their original bases unless forced to the next base by the new base runner.

If the ball hits the runner or umpire *after* touching any fielder, including the pitcher, the umpire should allow the ball to remain alive and in play. [Rules 6.08 (d), 6.09 (c), and 7.08 (f)]

XII. Obstruction and interference

As the football enthusiasts of the world like to point out, baseball is not really a contact sport. Unlike football, hockey, soccer, and basketball, baseball is a game where the players act on the ball; they usually do it without getting too involved with their opponents. They do not try to steal the ball from an opponent, like they do in soccer or basketball, and they do not try to block the opponent's throw or shot, like they do in football and basketball.

But contact occurs from time to time, and the umpire must make sure that one team does not gain an unfair advantage by getting in the way of an opponent. Making contact is sometimes legitimate—during a tag play at home plate, for example—but the umpire usually has to prevent players from interfering with each other's plays.

Obstruction and interference are birds of the same feather. Obstruction occurs when a *defensive player who is not making a play* impedes a base runner. Interference occurs when *any player who is involved in plays* makes illegal contact with opposing players. Both offensive and defensive players can be guilty of interference. [Rules 2.00, 5.09 (f), 6.05 (h,i,k), 6.08 (c), 7.04 (d), 7.06 (a,b), 7.08 (b,g), 7.09]

The umpire should ask himself several questions when players collide with each other. The key questions include: Should those players have collided? If they shouldn't have collided, who was at fault? What is the appropriate penalty? Where should the runners be placed? Is the ball alive or dead?

It's fairly easy to know who is at fault in an obstruction play— by definition it's the fielder. What to do with the players after the obstruction takes place is a little stickier. Here's what you should do in those cases:

When a fielder obstructs the batter-runner before he touches first, the umpire should call time out at the moment of obstruction. He should award the batter-runner at least first base. The other runners should advance one base if they would have been forced ahead when the batter-runner moved to first base. If the base runners are not affected by the batter-runner's progress, the umpire should place them according to how far he thinks they would have gotten if the obstruction had not occurred.

If a fielder obstructs a base runner on whom the defense is playing, the umpire should call time at the moment of obstruction. The obstructed runner should be awarded at least one base. Other runners should advance one base if they would be pushed that far by the obstructed runner's extra base. If they are not automatically advanced by the obstructed runner's advance, the umpire should place them according to his judgment. This play often develops during a rundown.

When any other obstruction occurs, the umpire should allow the play to be completed. The umpire should place the runners according to how he thinks they would have ended up without the obstruction.

XIII. Infield fly rule

The infield fly rule is the one rule that almost requires the umpire to act like a scout or a director of player evaluation. When the umpire invokes the infield fly rule, he must judge whether any of the fielders near a pop fly *has the ability to catch the ball.* That need to judge players' abilities makes the play very difficult for the umpire.

The infield fly rule should be invoked when a batter hits a ball high over the infield with no outs or one out, and with runners on first and second or the bases loaded. The umpire should invoke the rule when he thinks that a fielder can catch the fly with "ordinary effort." [Rules 2.00 infield fly and 6.05 (e)]

When the umpire calls an infield fly, the batter is automatically out and the runners can attempt to move to the next base only after tagging up, unless the ball is not caught.

The rule was written to protect offensive teams from being stuck in a Catch-22 situation when the batter hits a pop-up in a force-play situation. Because runners cannot advance on a fly ball unless they tag up, runners have to stay close to the base whenever the batter hits a high pop. Without the rule, fielders could allow easy pop-ups to fall to the ground, and still have time to force out the base-runners and maybe turn a double play.

The "ordinary effort" requirement is what makes the play so hard to call. A simple pop-up over the infield might be hard to catch because of the sun or the wind; if it is hard to catch, the umpire shouldn't call an infield fly. The umpire should be wary of infielders who try to make easy plays look hard.

The umpiring partners should alert each other when an infield fly situation exists. When the batter hits a fly ball that requires "ordinary effort," both umpires should holler: "Infield fly! The batter is out if the ball if fair!" The call should be made when the ball has reached its highest point and is about to fall.

XIV. Awards of bases to runners

The Detroit Tigers are playing the Baltimore Orioles in Detroit when the umpire makes a couple of apparently inconsistent calls that affect the game's outcome.

In the Tiger's first inning, the bases are loaded with one out when Barbaro Garbey hits a grounder to third base. The Orioles' third-baseman, Todd Cruz, heads for the bag but does not get there in time for the force play. He turns and throws the ball to first—but the ball goes into the stands. The umpire awards all runners two bases from the time of the throw. Since everyone was at his next base at the time of the throw, except the batter-runner, three runs score, and the batter-runner goes to second. [Rule 7.05ar play]

With the Orioles behind 3–0 in the top of the ninth, the situation is the same as it was in the first inning. Eddie Murray hits a shot deep to third base. Tiger third-baseman Darrell Evans fields the ball and, deciding right away he has no play at third, throws to first. Again, the ball goes into the stands. The umpire awards the runners two bases from the time of the pitch—allowing only two runs to score. Manager Joe Altobelli argues that his Orioles should get three runs like the Tigers got in the first inning. The O's end up losing 3–2. Altobelli protests the game. [Rule 7.05 (g)]

Altobelli will lose his protest because the plays were really quite different. The runners get two bases from the time of the throw if the infielder's throw is not the first play by an infielder—but only two bases from the time of the pitch if the infielder's throw was the first play by an infielder. Cruz first went for a force at third base, while Evans went to first right away.

Here's how this rule works for other situations:

The runners get *two bases from the time of the pitch* when:

- As in our Evans example above, the fielder throws the ball into dead territory on the first play by an infielder. [Rule 7.05 (h)ar]
- The fielder deflects a wild pitch into dead territory when retrieving the ball. The catcher will usually be the culprit here. [Rule 7.05 (h)]
- A batted ball bounces over or flies through the outfield fence. This is the typical ground-rule double. [Rule 7.05 (f)]

- A fair ball is deflected into dead territory from foul territory. This happens when the outfielder tries to track a hit down the line and accidentally hits the ball into the stands. [Rule 7.05 (f)]

The runners get *two bases from the time of the throw* when:

- Any relay is thrown into dead territory. This usually happens when an outfielder throws the ball toward third to cut down a runner, and the ball gets away. [Rule 7.05 (f)]
- A ball is thrown into dead territory by a player without the ball being hit. This happens when the catcher throws the ball away on a pickoff attempt at first or third base. [Rule 7.05 (g)]
- The ball is thrown into dead territory on a "subsequent" play. [Rule 7.05ar] This is what happened in our Cruz example above: his throw was not the first play by an infielder, so the runners got two bases from the time of the throw. [Rule 7.05 (g)ar]
- The ball is thrown into dead territory after the batter and all runners have all already advanced one base. [Rule 7.05 (g)ar]

XV. Appeals

An appeal play takes place whenever a player on the defensive team tells the umpire that an offensive player:

- Failed to touch a base as he moved around the bases.
- Failed to tag up at a base before advancing to the next base on a fly ball. [Rules 7.08 (d,k), 7.10]

In an appeal play, the defensive team must either tag the base runner or touch the base that the base runner missed or failed to tag up on. The appeal play must take place when the ball is alive. An appeal can be made only before the next pitch, play, or attempted play.

The defensive team can make only one appeal play on a given runner at a given base. If the defensive team throws the ball into the stands while attempting an appeal play, it may not try to make an appeal on that runner at that base again.

A defensive team can make appeals in all instances when a base runner might have missed a base or failed to tag up on a fly ball. If the defense thinks that a runner missed two bases, or that more than one base runner missed a base, the defense can make appeals on all of those plays.

In a continuous action play, a team could end up recording as many as four outs in an inning—and then choose which outs it would like to have count.

Suppose the St. Louis Cardinals are playing the Pittsburgh Pirates. Ozzie Smith is on second base and Willie McGee is on first for the Cardinals with two outs. Andy Van Slyke hits a blooping single to right field. Smith scores, and McGee is thrown out trying to advance to third. The putout of McGee represents the third out of the inning, but the run still counts. The Pirates, however, contend Smith missed third base on his way home, and they appeal the play. They win the appeal—which means that play was the third out of the inning and the run doesn't count.

The appeal play is considered a regular play—which means that the team making the appeal play must assume all the risks of a regular play, such as the possibility of throwing the ball away or allowing another base runner to steal a base.

When an appeal results in the third out of the inning . . .   Occasionally, a defensive team will record the third out of an inning on an appeal play—when a defensive player touches a base that a base runner failed to touch on his way around the basepaths. If a run is scored during the play that the defense successfully appeals, the umpire will have to determine how many runs, if any, should count. [Rules 4.09 (a) and 7.12]

- If the successful appeal play takes place at a base that the batter-runner or runner was forced to, no runs score. If a runner on first base misses second base—where he could be forced out on a ground ball—the appeal play should be treated like a force play. Since force plays are not time plays, no runs score.

- If the successful appeal takes place at first base, no runs score. If the batter-runner is put out before first base, no runs can score.

- If the successful appeal takes place under any other circumstances, the runners ahead of the appealed runner score, the appealed runner does not score, and the runners behind the appealed runner do not score.

XVI. Batting out of order

When a batter bats out of his turn in the lineup, confusion reigns. [Rule 6.07]

An umpire involved in a lineup mixup will be barraged with questions. Should a team that fails to honor the lineup be allowed to "keep" a hit? Can the umpires and the managers from both teams stay mum about the mixup even if they know about it? Can the umpire deprive a batter of his turn at the plate because his teammate hit out of turn? Can a hitter run up an unfavorable count during a turn at the plate, then turn that count over to a teammate who should have been hitting?

The answer to all of these questions is "yes." Let's see why.

The umpire's responsibilities in policing the lineup rule vary from league to league. In professional baseball, the umpire is not supposed to do anything if batters are hitting out of order, even if he notices that something is wrong, until one of the team's managers brings the problem to his attention.

What an improper batter does "stands" or "counts" when the *defensive team makes any kind of play after that batter's improper turn at the plate*. If a batter bats before his proper place in the lineup, and if the pitcher throws a pitch to the next batter, what the first batter did counts. Likewise, if an improper batter's turn is followed by a play such as a pickoff attempt, the improper batter's turn counts.

If anyone is called out as a result of a team's hitting out of order, it is the proper batter—the person who, by not appearing at the plate as soon as he should, got the team in the mess.

Here are the situations the umpire might have to deal with when a team forgets about its batting order:

- If the mixup is discovered after the improper batter completes his turn at bat but before the next pitch or play, the proper batter is out. If any base runners advanced to another base as a result of the improper batter's action, they are sent back to their original bases.

  The next batter in such cases is the batter whose name follows the proper batter's name in the lineup. This rule, just or unjust, deprives the man who is listed before the improper batter of a turn at bat.

- If the proper batter is on base when the problem is discovered, the umpire will allow him to remain as a base runner. His name will be passed over, and the proper batter is the man whose name follows his in the batter order.

- If the appeal is made before the improper batter completes his at-bat, the proper batter will finish the at-bat with the same count. All base runners' advances are legal.

- If the appeal on an improper batter is made after a pitch or play on the subsequent batter, the improper batter and his actions become legalized; all runners' advances are legal. The batting order should pick up with the batter whose name follows the legalized improper batter in the lineup.

XVII. The designated hitter rule

The designated hitter rule allows a manager to substitute an offensive player in the lineup for a weak-hitting member of the team. The rule is one of the most controversial developments in baseball's recent history because it takes away from the game's purity. Baseball's traditionalists argue that the game should require players to possess a wide range of skills. With this rule, pitchers need not know how to hold a bat and some sluggers need not know how to put on a glove. The rule was adopted by the American League for one reason—to lure fans to ballparks with the prospect of greater displays of hitting.

Whatever its advantages or drawbacks, the rule appears to have become a permanent part of baseball at all levels. Almost all organized baseball leagues use the rule. [Rule 6.10]

Some leagues allow a designated hitter to hit for any weak-hitting part of the lineup. In Little League and high-school baseball, the pitcher is often one of the better hitters on the team. The manager might then use the designated hitter for the shortstop or center fielder who is put into the lineup because of his defensive skills.

Several rules have been devised to govern the extra player, including:

- The designated hitter rule is optional. No team is required to substitute an offensive player for the pitcher in the batting order, but the team must start the game with a designated hitter if that team intends to use a D.H. at all during the game. It's a use-it-or-lose-it situation.

- The first designated hitter must bat at least one time unless there is a pitcher change. This rule was developed in response to a trick employed by Earl Weaver. In the early days of the rule, Weaver put a player into the lineup who he knew would not play in the game—the previous game's pitcher, for example —and then "substituted" for that player when he found out which pitcher would be working for the opposing team.

- A pinch hitter or pinch runner for the designated hitter becomes the designated hitter's replacement.

- The pitcher is a defensive player only; the designated hitter is an offensive player only.

- The designated hitter is locked in the same position in the batting order for the entire game.

- If a team decides to use its pitcher offensively, the pitcher may bat only for the designated hitter.

- If a designated hitter is ejected from a game, his manager does not need to announce his replacement until his spot in the lineup comes up.

- A team loses its rights to use the designated hitter when: 1) the player who starts the game as the designated hitter takes a defensive position, 2) the pitcher bats for the designated hitter, 3) another defensive player moves to the pitching position, 4) a pinch-hitter comes in to pitch, or 5) a pitcher goes to another defensive position.

XVIII. Different leagues, different rules

Every organized baseball league follows the basic form of the Official Baseball Rules, but the leagues differ on some important details. The rules variations usually stem from the different objectives that the leagues' organizers have for their players. Little League and high-school leagues put an emphasis on safety and fun rather than serious competition. College and professional players are older and more responsible—and often have more at stake in a game—so their leagues give the players a little more leeway on safety issues but make more technical distinctions on rule interpretations. For example, a college batter will be called out automatically if he steps to the plate without a helmet; a professional player will simply be told to fetch a helmet. Before you begin work in a league, you should get a copy of that league's rule differences.

Some of the major rule differences follow:

Appeals. High-school leagues require the umpire to call a runner out when he commits a base-running infraction. College and professional umpires ignore the infraction until a defensive player makes an appeal.

Base on balls. High-school pitchers may grant the batter an intentional walk without throwing the ball. College and professional pitchers must throw four balls for the batter to be granted a free pass.

The batter. If a high-school player delays stepping into the batter's box for twenty seconds, the umpire should call an automatic strike. That automatic strike will be called in college ball when the player fails to enter the box upon the umpire's orders. When a batter delays getting into the box in the pros, the umpire should tell the pitcher to throw the ball anyway—and then call each pitch a strike.

The batter must have both feet *entirely* in the box before the pitcher can pitch in high-school leagues. College and professional leagues require only that *parts* of both feet be in the box. If the batter leaves the box during the pitch in high school or professional ball, the umpire's call on the pitch depends on where the pitch lands in relation to the strike zone. In college and Little League ball, it's an automatic strike when the batter leaves the box.

Designated hitter rule. Most amateur leagues allow teams to use a designated hitter for any fielder, while the pros and college allow a D.H. only for the pitcher.

Equipment. The professional leagues require batters to use wooden bats, while amateur leagues allow aluminum bats. Leagues differ from area to area on the standards for giving the bat a good grip.

Little League and high-school leagues usually require the catcher to put on as much protective equipment as possible— including helmet, shin guards, body protector, a mask with a protective throat guard, and a protective cup. Colleges require the helmet and throat guard, and the pros make no rules provision.

Metal cleats are forbidden in Little League and high school, but are allowed in college and pro ball.

The batter and the on-deck hitter must wear protective helmets with two earflaps in Little League and high school. Only the batter and runner are required to wear the helmet in college and pro leagues.

Obstruction. Obstruction is always treated as a delayed dead ball in high-school leagues. But in college and professional baseball, the ball is immediately dead if the batter-runner is obstructed before he reaches first base or if the defense is playing on the obstructed runner. A fake tag is an obstruction in high-school baseball, but not in college or pro ball.

Pitcher. When the pitcher balks in high-school leagues, the ball is immediately dead. Any play that follows the balk is nullified, and the balk ruling is enforced (each runner gets one base). In the college and professional leagues the balk is ignored when the players advance at least one base during the play. If, for example, a batter hits a home run on a balked pitch in high school, the home run is nullified and the balk is enforced. That homer would count in college and professional baseball.

If the umpire finds that the ball is doctored in any way but cannot determine who is responsible, the umpire should hold the pitcher responsible in professional leagues. There is no rule provision for this situation for other leagues.

Pitchers must take the signs from the catcher while standing on the rubber. Pitchers who fail to follow this rule in high school ball get a ball or balk called. College pitchers get a ball called, and pro pitchers just get a warning.

If a pitcher throws at a batter in Little League or high-school competition, he can be ejected from the game. College and pro pitchers have to be warned before they can be ejected.

Scoring. Little League and high-school leagues often have a ten-run rule, in which the game is declared over if one team takes a ten-run lead after five innings. College and professional leagues have no such provision.

Amateur leagues sometimes adopt "speed-up" rules designed to prevent players from slowing the pace of the game. The pros don't.

Substitutions. Little League and high-school leagues allow players to reenter the game after they have left if they return to the same spot in the batting lineup. Colleges and pros don't allow players to return to the game.

Little League and high-school team managers or coaches must tell the umpire when they bring substitutes into the game. College and professional leagues make a substitution official when the player takes his position.

Umpire authority.   The plate umpire doesn't have to ask for help from his partner on a check-swing call in Little League or high-school games. That umpire does have to get help when the catcher or coach asks for it in college and pro games.

TEN
Test Your Knowledge of Umpiring

Baseball can be as simple or complex a contest as the viewer wants it to be. Not to slight the game's potential for exquisite strategy, we umpires usually prefer the game to be as straightforward as possible, thank you.

For the knowledgeable fan, the game's riveting strategy is almost always below the surface; for the umpire, that strategy is, thankfully, almost always out of sight. The umpire does not need to get involved in the intense battle of wits between pitcher and hitter, in the pinch-hitting and relief-pitching strategies of the managers, or in the positioning of fielders or running strategies.

The umpire just has to make the calls as he sees the plays, collect his money, go home, and have a nice glass of iced tea.

Pretty simple, eh? Well, sort of, once you have mastered the fundamental mechanics and the rules of the game. But things can get difficult. There will be plenty of times where the umpire has to string rules together or decide which of two or three contradicting rules apply to a specific play. Those are the times that test umpires' powers of reasoning and quickness and, of course, nerves.

Here's a quick way to test your knowledge of the rules. Each answer references the rule number. Review the previous chapter and the baseball rulebook for the topics of the questions you miss on this quiz.

The answers appear at the end of the quiz. Note that there might be more than one answer to some questions.

1. With a man on third base, the batter fouls the ball straight back to the catcher. The ball hits the catcher's shin guard, though, and bounces away. The runner on third comes in to score. The defensive team protests that the runner should return to third base because the foul makes the ball dead. How should you rule?

2. The pitcher throws an 0-and-2 pitch to the batter. The batter swings and misses. The pitch hits the catcher's shin guards and bounces high in the air just in front of the plate. The catcher grabs the ball before it touches anything else. What should the umpire call?

a. A foul tip and the batter is out.

b. A foul ball and the batter continues to hit with the 0-and-2 count.

c. Strike three and the batter is out.

d. Strike three, but the batter must be tagged out or thrown out at first base.

3. The umpires invoke the infield fly rule when the batter hits a pop fly near the outer edge of the infield dirt. An outfielder misses the ball, but the umpires still call the batter out because of the infield fly ruling. The batter complains that the infield fly rule should not have been invoked since the outfielder clearly was the fielder responsible for the ball. Can the umpire call the infield fly when an outfielder is involved, or must an infielder be involved in the play?

4. A manager brings in a relief pitcher, and the reliever runs the count to 3-and-2. The manager decides to bring in another pitcher. As the new pitcher warms up on the mound, the umpire realizes that the first reliever did not pitch to one complete batter. What should the umpire do?

a. Require the first relief pitcher to return and finish pitching to the batter.

b. Allow the new pitcher to stay in the game, and keep the count at 3-and-2.

5. A pinch hitter bats for the catcher, who is batting in the fifth spot of the lineup. The pinch hitter stays in the game at third base.

The previous third baseman batted fourth. Another substitute enters the game as the catcher. Where does the catcher bat in the lineup?

6. Does an umpire have to honor a pitcher's request for a new ball? Does the umpire have to honor the batter's request for a new ball?

7. When a game is protested, which of the following procedures should an umpire follow?
  a. Ask his partner if he agrees with the decision.
  b. Announce the protest to the opposing manager.
  c. Announce the protest to the spectators.
  d. Ask the opposing manager if he also would protest the game if the umpires agree with the first manager's protest.
  e. Make note of the exact situation at the time of the protest.
  f. Offer the protesting manager the option of doing the play over—if both managers agree.

8. Rain causes the umpire to hold up a game in the seventh inning with the home team ahead, 4–3. During the rain delay, the lights fail. The rain stops and the field is playable, but the lights cannot be fixed. What should the umpire do?
  a. Suspend the game, and resume it another day with the same game situation that existed at the time of the rain delay.
  b. Call the game because of the light failure, with the home team winning 4–3.
  c. Call the game because of rain, with the home team winning 4–3.

9. There are two outs and the bases are loaded. The batter hits a home run. How many runs score in the following situations?
  a. The runner from second base is called out on an appeal for missing third base.
  b. The runner from second base is called out on an appeal for missing home plate.
  c. The runner from first base is called out on an appeal for missing third base.
  d. The runner from first base is called out on an appeal for missing home plate.

e. The batter-runner is called out on an appeal for missing second base.

f. The batter-runner is called out on an appeal for missing first base.

10.　There are two outs and a runner on second base. The batter hits a ball into the right-center field alley. Does the run count in the following two situations?

a. The batter-runner is called out trying to stretch the hit into a double after the runner crosses home plate.

b. The batter-runner is called out at second base before the runner crosses home plate.

11.　There are two outs and a runner on second base. The base runner unintentionally runs into a ground ball which the third baseman, playing in for a bunt, tried to field and brushed with his glove only a split second before. The shortstop might have had a play but now must be content to chase the ball down. Is the ball dead or alive? If the ball is dead, where should the umpire place the runners and should the umpire call anyone out on the play?

12.　There are two outs with runners on first and third. The pitch gets by the catcher and gets stuck in the umpire's mask. The runners were not attempting a steal on the play. Is the ball dead or alive? If the ball is dead, where should the umpire place the runners and should the umpire call anyone out on the play?

13.　There is a man on second base attempting to steal when a batter gets hit with the pitch. Is the ball dead or alive? If the ball is dead, where should the umpire place the runners and should the umpire call anyone out on the play?

14.　What is the proper procedure for putting a ball into play?

15.　With a 0-and-2 count on him, the batter refuses to get set in the batter's box. The umpire orders the pitcher to ignore the batter and to throw a pitch. The pitcher throws the ball, and the umpire immediately calls strike three. But the ball gets away, and the runner beats the catcher's throw to first base. What should the umpire do?

16. After the batter bunts a ball into fair territory, he races down the first base line in fair territory. He collides with the first baseman, who is taking a throw from the pitcher. The first baseman drops the ball. Should the umpire call the batter out for interference?

17. A batter swings at a ball when he has one foot out of the batter's box. Should the umpire call him out if he hits the ball foul? What if he misses the ball?

18. There are two outs and a runner on second base in the top of the ninth inning. The visiting team is on the short end of a 5–4 game. The catcher interferes with the batter's swing, but the batter manages to single to left field anyway. The center fielder then cuts down the runner as he attempts to score—and the game is apparently over. But the visiting team's manager tells the umpire he wants him to call interference on the catcher—which would put the runner back at second base and the batter-runner at first base with two outs. How should the umpire rule?

19. Does catcher's interference kill the ball at the moment the interference takes place?

20. The batter hits a long fly ball, which an outfielder deflects over the outfield fence into foul territory. Where should the runner be placed? What if the outfielder deflected the ball over the fence in fair territory?

21. Batter B bats in Batter A's spot in the batting order. He has a 2-and-2 count on him when the defensive team's manager appeals the order of hitters. What happens?
    a. Batter A is out.
    b. Batter B is out.
    c. Batter A takes over at the plate with a 2-and-2 count.
    d. Batter B continues to bat with a 2-and-2 count. When he finished the at-bat, the umpire orders the next proper batter to the plate. If Batter B singles, Batter A takes his place at first base and B takes another turn at the plate.

22. Which of the following events would end a team's right to use the designated hitter?

    a. Replacing the designated hitter with a pinch hitter or pinch runner.

    b. The pitcher moves to another defensive position.

    c. Another defensive player moves in to pitch.

    d. The designated hitter is called out as a result of a play in which someone batted out of order.

    e. A pinch hitter or pinnch runner enters the game to pitch.

    f. The designated hitter is ejected by the umpire.

    g. The pitcher bats for the designated hitter.

    h. The designated hitter enters the game defensively.

    i. A relief pitcher enters the game to pitch.

23. The batter hits a single to right field. The right fielder throws to first in an attempt to retire the batter-runner, who took too wide a turn at first. The ball goes into the dugout. When the ball went into the dugout, the runner was just past second base. Place the runner.

24. There's one out and a runner on first base attempts to steal. The catcher interferes with the batter, who strikes out, and then throws the runner out at second base. What should the umpire do?

25. There's one out and a runner on first base. The pitcher balks as he attempts to pick off the runner, and he throws the ball past the first baseman and into the right-field corner. The runner races all the way to third base, but he misses second base. The shortstop steps on second base in an appeal of the play, and the umpire calls the runner out. The offensive team's manager protests the decision. He claims the runner was entitled to second base because of the balk and should be placed there. Who is right?

26. There is one out with runners on second and third base. From a set position, the pitcher steps toward third base and fakes a throw. Now off the rubber, he turns around and throws to second base to pick off the runner standing nearby. Is the runner at second base out?

27. There are no outs, a runner at second base, and a 3-and-2 count on the batter. On the next pitch, the pitcher throws a grease-ball, which the batter swings at and misses. What should the umpire do?

> a. Warn the pitcher, move the runner to third base, and call the batter out on strikes.
> b. Eject the pitcher, leave the runner on second base, and call a ball four on the batter.
> c. Warn the pitcher, leave the runner on second base, and call a ball four on the batter.
> d. Warn the pitcher, move the runner to third base, and call ball four on the batter.

28. With a runner on first base, the batter grounds the ball sharply to first base. The first baseman steps on the bag. As he throws the ball to second base, the base runner sprints back to first base. He easily beats the throw to first base. The first baseman protests that the runner must attempt to reach second base, and is not allowed to run the bases backwards. What happens?

29. As the batter jumps out of the batter's box to avoid getting hit with a pitch, the ball hits his bat and bounces in front of the plate. The catcher grabs the ball and throws to first base. Is the batter out or should the umpire call the pitch a ball?

30. The catcher interferes with the batter's swing but the batter still manages to hit a triple down the third-base line. The defense immediately appeals the play, claiming that the batter-runner failed to touch first base, and the umpire agrees. The batter-runner then says that, as part of the option play, he'd like to go to first base because of catcher's interference. Should the umpire let him go to first base, or call him out on the appeal play?

31. There's a base runner on first base with one out, and the first baseman is playing ahead of the base in anticipation of a sacrifice bunt. The batter swings away. When the base runner is halfway to second base, he is struck with the batted ball, which then bounces into foul territory. By the time the fielders retrieve the ball, the base runners have reached second and third base. How should the umpires place the runners? How many outs are there?

32. There's a runner on first base with a 2-and-2 count with two outs when the umpire calls the next pitch a strike. The catcher misses the ball, the batter runs toward first base, and the runner darts for second base on the third strike. The catcher's throw to second base easily beats the runner. Should the runner be called out on a force play?

33. With a runner on first base and one out, the batter hits a long fly ball to the left-center field alley. The center fielder runs a long way and finally catches the ball—and he crashes into the wall, where he is knocked unconscious and falls to the ground. The runner at first base, seeing the center fielder lying on the ground, dashes all the way home to score. The left fielder takes the ball out of his teammate's glove and throws it to first base. The umpire calls the batter out on the fly ball and the runner out for not tagging up before scoring. The offensive team argues that the outfielder did not have complete control of the ball and therefore did not legally catch it—and that the run should count with no outs on the play. Who's right?

34. Same play as above. The offensive manager argues that the ball should be declared dead when it became obvious that the outfielder was knocked unconscious. Is that true?

35. In the middle of his turn at the plate, a batter decides he'll get a better view of the pitches from the other side of the plate— so he moves to the batter's box on the other side of the plate. The defense complains that the umpire should call the batter out for not first calling time out. Should the batter be called out?

36. There's a runner on first base when the catcher starts to throw the ball to the pitcher after a pitch. The umpire accidentally hits the catcher's arm as the catcher throws the ball, and the ball bounces into foul territory. What happens if the base runner breaks for second base and beats the throw? What if he's called out?

37. With the bases loaded, one out, and a full count on the batter, the manager for the offensive team gambles: he flashes the steal sign for all base runners. The runner from third base, trying to score home, is hit with the pitch, which cuts through the strike zone. The catcher grabs the ball, and throws the ball to third base, where the throw is in plenty of time to beat the runner from second base. How should the umpires deal with this mess?

Answers

1. The ball is a foul ball, not a foul tip, so the ball is dead. For a ball to be called a foul tip, it must go "sharp and direct from the bat to the *catcher's hands* and be caught." The ball here hit the catcher's shin guard. Since it's a foul ball, the base runner must return to his original base. *Rule 2.00 foul ball.*

2. C. Since the batter missed the ball, it's strike three. If the catcher missed the ball, the runner could try to beat a throw to first base. But he caught the ball, so there's no play at first. *Rule 2.00 catch.*

3. The infield fly rule requires only that the ball be hit over the infield and that a fielder can make the catch with ordinary effort. Whether an infielder or an outfielder makes the play is unimportant. *Rule 2.00 infield fly.*

4. A. The pitcher must pitch to at least one complete batter unless he gets hurt. *Rule 3.05 (b) (c).*

5. The new catcher will bat fourth. Two players who enter the game at the same time can bat in either of the batting slots opened by the players who left the game. *Rule 3.03.*

6. Yes and no. *Rules 3.01 (e) and 3.01.*

7. A, B, C, E. The umpire should not go around asking for opinions from any coaches or players. He is on the field to make the decisions himself. *Rule 4.19.*

8. A. If the rain delay caused the game to be called, the game would end with the score for the last full inning of play. But mechanical delays such as light failure—which could be caused by the overeager home team management—should result in a suspended game. *Rule 4.12 (a).*

9.   0, 1, 2, 2, 3, and 0. What matters is the position of the base runners at the time of the inning's third out. *Rule 4.09 (a) and 7.12.*

10.   Yes and no. It's a time play, and the umpires have to make a judgment call. *Rule 4.09 (a).*

11.   The ball is alive because the fielder had a chance to field the ball in front of the runner. *Rule 5.09 (f).*

12.   The ball is dead. The runners should be sent to home and second base. *Rule 5.09 (g).*

13.   The ball is dead when it hits the batter. The batter should be awarded first base, and the runner should be sent back to his original base unless forced to advance. *Rule 5.09 (a).*

14.   Order the pitcher to stand on the rubber with the ball, and shout: "Play!" *Rule 5.11.*

15.   Call the batter out on strikes. This is a legitimate way of preventing delay of game. *Rule 6.02 (c).*

16.   Yes, because he adversely affected the first baseman's ability to complete a play. *Rule 6.05 (k).*

17.   Yes and no. For the umpire to make an "illegally *batted* ball" call, the ball must be hit. If the batter does hit the ball, it's an out. *Rule 6.06 (a).*

18.   The play stands because it is not an option play. It ceases to be interference when the batter reaches first base and the runners advance at least one base. *Rules 6.08 (c) and 7.04 (d).*

19.   Not necessarily. There might be a delayed dead ball situation or an option play. *Rule 6.08 (c).*

20.   Ground-rule double and home run. *Rule 6.09 (h).*

21.   C. The proper batter should always complete the at-bat if the mistake is discovered before the end of the at-bat. *Rule 6.07.*

22. B, C, E, G, H. *Rule 6.10.*

23. He gets third because he gets two bases from the time of the throw. The key here is to determine where the runner was at the time of the throw. *Rule 7.05 (g).*

24. The catcher's interference affected the whole play. The ball is dead, and the batter gets first base. The base runner advances to second base because he's forced there. *Rule 7.04 (d).*

25. The umpire. Even when a player is entitled to a base, he still has to touch it. Silly, silly manager! *Rule 8.05.*

26. Yes. The ball is always in play here. *Rule 8.05 (c).*

27. C. Unless the umpire actually discovers proof of tampering with the ball, he must give the pitcher a warning before he ejects him. The runner is not forced to third base, but a ball is called. *Rule 8.02.*

28. The runner is safe at first. He can return to first base since there's not a force play anymore. *Rules 2.00 and 7.08 (e).*

29. He's out. Even if he didn't mean to, the batter hit the ball. He's responsible for that. *Rules 2.00, 6.09 (a), 6.05 (j).*

30. He's out. The option play doesn't exist if the batter got at least as far as first base. *Rule 6.08 (c).*

31. The runners stay where they are with no outs on the play because the fielder was ahead of the runner when the runner was hit. *Rule 6.09 (c).*

32. Yes. With two outs and a runner on first base, the batter must try to go to first base—forcing the runner to try for second base. *Rule 6.09 (b).*

33. The umpire is right. The center fielder had complete possession of the ball when he went down. *Rule 2.00.*

34. The ball is not dead until the play is completed. *Rule 5.10 (h).*

35. No. The batter can switch batter's boxes as long as he does it before the pitcher gets set on the mound to throw the ball. *Rules 6.02 (b) and 6.06 (b).*

36. If the catcher can get the runner despite the umpire's interference, the out will count. If he cannot get the runner, the umpire should order him back to his original base. *Rule 5.09 (b).*

37. The runner scores, the batter strikes out, the ball is dead, and the other runners are advanced one base. *Rules 5.09 (h) and 6.05 (n).*

ELEVEN
Umpiring Softball Games

Modern baseball's indoor stadiums, such as the Astrodome in Houston and the Hubert H. Humphrey Metrodome in Minneapolis, do not represent the first attempts of baseball lovers to take their sport away from inclement weather.

The establishment of softball back in the nineteenth century was the first attempt to bring baseball indoors.

According to legend, Thanksgiving Day in 1887 was the day the game of softball was invented. Frustrated with a cold rain that prohibited a holiday game of baseball, one George W. Hancock of the Farragut Boat Club in Chicago modified the rules of baseball so that some local youngsters would have something to do during the holiday afternoon. The youngsters played the game in the boat club's gymnasium all afternoon.

The new game gained popularity quickly. A member of the Minneapolis Fire Department is credited with bringing softball outdoors in 1895. A group of softball enthusiasts got together in 1932 to form the Amateur Softball Association of America. Because of the larger ball, smaller field, and less dangerous pitching, the game caught on among all ages and both sexes. Today softball is the most popular participation sport in America—millions play in formal leagues every spring and summer.

Obviously, an organized sport of such popularity needs umpires. Fortunately for the baseball umpire, the differences between baseball and softball are so slight that any baseball umpire can become a good softball umpire.

Size of the field and apparent speed of the ball are the crucial differences between baseball and softball. The softball field is smaller than the baseball field. The softball is bigger than the baseball. And the softball pitch seems, depending on the rules you use, either much faster or much slower.

The two-man umpiring system works for softball as well as baseball. But the game requires that the field umpire take different positions when he covers the bases.

With no base runners, the field umpire takes the same position as he would working a baseball game. He stands on the right-field line, about fifteen feet beyond the first baseman.

But the softball umpire parts company with the baseball umpire when the team at bat has base runners. Rather than standing *in front* and to one side of second base, the softball umpire stands *behind* and to one side of the base.

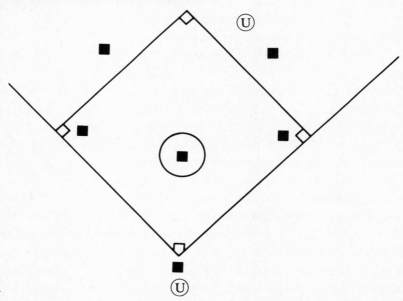

The field umpire in softball stands behind rather than in front of second base with base runners on board. If he stood in front of the bag, like the baseball umpire, he'd not only get in the way of players, he'd also have a poor view of both the batter and base runner.

Standing to the outfield side of the base is a practical matter. Because a softball field is so much smaller, the umpire would constantly get in the players' way if he took the inside position. There would be all kinds of bumping, ball-kicking, and obstruction of players' views. There just isn't room for both players and umpires in the infield.

Also, because the field is so small, the umpire needs to stand back a bit to get a good view of plays. The softball is often hit hard, and the umpire needs all the time and as much of a visual field as he can get. The farther back he can get, the larger the view of the diamond he will have.

Standing back also enables the field umpire to enforce softball's base running rules. Base runners in fast-pitch softball leagues are not allowed to leave their bases until the pitcher releases the ball, and runners in slow-pitch leagues must hold until the pitch reaches the plate. The only way the umpire can see all the important players at once is to stand back and line up the players in one picture.

The umpire moves into the diamond on plays in the outfield so he can see both the runners and the outfielders and he doesn't have to run himself crazy to get to all the plays.

The plate umpire assumes virtually the same position in softball as baseball. How he will concentrate on the pitches is a different matter, but we'll get to that later.

Here are the basic rules for the various types of softball, and how the umpire should go about enforcing those rules.

The players, field dimensions, equipment

The aim of the game and the shape of the field are basically the same as baseball. But a few rule modifications change in many significant ways how coaches and players approach the game. Among the differences:

The game. Most regulation softball games last seven innings. Most games will be considered officially completed after four innings if the game must then be halted because of inclement weather or scheduling conflicts or other problems.

Players. Like baseball, fast-pitch softball allows the use of nine players and, depending on the league, a designated hitter. Slow-pitch softball allows ten players. The additional player, the "short-fielder," is stationed in the shallow outfield area behind second base.

Both brands of softball allow the manager to make substitutions for the starting players and later in the game put the starter back into the game. The removed starter must assume his old position in the batting order, but he may play any position.

Dimensions. Fast-pitch games are played on diamonds with sixty feet between the bases, and forty-six feet from the mound to the plate in men's leagues and forty feet from the mound to the plate in women's leagues.

The bases are sixty-five feet apart in men's slow-pitch leagues and sixty feet apart in women's leagues.

Minimum distances to the outfield fences vary greatly from league to league. Whereas baseball requires 320 feet down the lines, fast-pitch softball requires 225, and slow-pitch requires 275, 250, or 225, depending on the league.

Equipment. Fast-pitch leagues sometimes require the batter and catcher to wear helmets and the catcher to wear some kind of chest protector. Catchers and umpires must wear masks in most organizations. Besides that, no protective equipment is necessary.

The glove a fielder may use is often restricted by individual league rules. Usually, all players but the catcher and first baseman must use small gloves. The exact size specifications vary.

Hitters may not use bats longer than 34 inches, heavier than thirty-eight ounces, or fatter than 2¼ inches in most leagues. Most leagues allow aluminum as well as wood bats. The kinds of substances batters may use to improve their grips vary.

The size of the balls varies from 12 inches, give or take ⅛ inch, in most fast- and slow-pitch competition, to 16 inches, give or take ¼ inch, in slow-pitch competition.

Pitching

In baseball, the umpire's inspection of the pitcher's motion usually is an afterthought. The umpire looks out, from time to time, for balks and other illegal pitches. Rarely does he have to make judgments about the legality of the pitcher's motion. The softball umpire has to make those on practically each pitch. This is the major difference between umpiring baseball and softball.

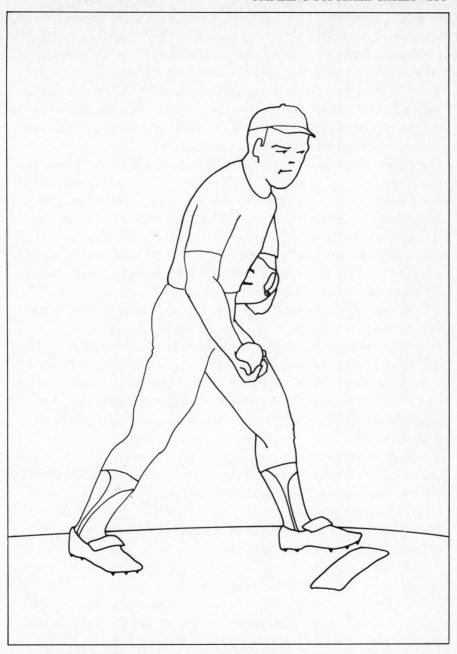

You have to judge the pitcher's motion on every pitch of the game. In fast-pitch competition, the pitcher must release the ball with his hand below the waist and with his hand as close to his body as his elbow.

Fast-pitch softball. Fast-pitch pitchers must begin each pitch by standing with both feet on the rubber. After getting the signal from the catcher, the pitcher must hold the ball with both hands for one to ten seconds, wind up, and throw the ball.

The most important thing for the umpire to watch—since most pitchers will instinctively follow the rules for the pitching motion —is the pitcher's hands and arms. How the pitcher uses his hand and arm will affect the pitch's speed.

The pitcher must release the ball with his hands below the waist, and his wrist must be at least as close to his body as his elbow. Both rules are designed to prevent the pitcher from throwing sidearm in instead of underhand. Allowing the pitcher to sneak in sidearm pitches paralyzes the batter, who already has a tough time handling the fast pitch from such a short distance.

The pitcher may swing his arm around in a "windmill" to get more speed on the pitch.

When he releases the ball, the fast-pitch pitcher must follow through with a motion toward home plate.

If the pitcher is guilty of an illegal pitch—bouncing the ball to the plate, using an illegal motion, doctoring the ball, or throwing to a base without stepping off the rubber—the umpire should call a ball and allow any base runners to advance one base.

Slow-pitch softball. Judging the arc is the key to umpiring slow-pitch softball.

Slow-pitch softball was designed to be a more leisurely pastime than fast-pitch. Whereas batting averages in fast-pitch competition rarely exceed .100, football-like scores and "tater contests" (long-ball hitting) dominate slow-pitch competition. People of all ages—and in all kinds of physical condition—feel comfortable taking part in slow-pitch competition.

All pitches in slow-pitch ball must rise between six and twelve feet above the ground on the way to home plate. That sounds like a simple rule to enforce until you realize how crafty some pitchers can be. Most slow-pitch pitchers try to get the ball to drop into the strike zone at different places and angles depending on the batter. That means the arc reaches its height at different spots between the mound and the plate.

The umpire must make a subjective judgment of the pitch's speed as well as its arc. Each pitch must be of "moderate" speed,

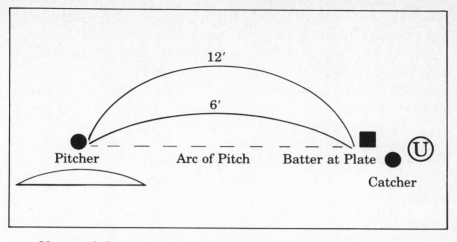

Slow-pitch leagues require the pitcher to throw the ball at an arc of between six and twelve feet between the mound and home plate.

the rulebooks say. The definition of moderate varies from league to league. Ask league officials for hints on judging the speed in your league.

The slow-pitch hurler also must comply with rules for the windup and motion. He must start and complete each pitch with at least one foot—usually the pivot foot—on the rubber. He can hold the ball with one or two hands for up to ten seconds before going into his motion. He must move forward as he releases the ball, and his feet can't move beyond the length of the rubber. Throughout the pitch, the pitcher's shoulders must be in line with first and third base, and his hand should be below his hip when he releases the ball.

Offense and the strike zone

As I said in my discussion of the baseball umpire's duties behind the plate, strike zones vary from league to league according to the talent of the players. The same goes for softball.

As a general rule, the strike zone for fast-pitch competition is between the batter's armpits and knees. In slow-pitch softball, the zone is expanded to include the area between the shoulders and knees. Any pitch that cuts any part of the strike zone is a strike; other pitches are balls.

Batters may bunt in fast-pitch leagues, but not slow-pitch

leagues. If the slow-pitch batter tries to bunt or hit the ball directly down into the infield, he should be called out.

Runners can leave the base after the pitcher releases the ball in fast-pitch competition and when the pitch reaches the plate in slow-pitch competition. Runners who leave the base early should be called out.

Because no runners are allowed to lead, the pitcher doesn't make any pickoff attempts—and the umpire doesn't have to worry about balks.